VINTAGE McCLURE

Robert B. McClure
with
Diane Forrest

WELCH PUBLISHING COMPANY INC.
Burlington, Ontario, Canada

Canadian Cataloguing in Publication Data

McClure, Robert B. (Robert Baird), 1900-
    Vintage McClure

ISBN 1-55011-055-1

1. Church and social problems. I. Forrest, Diane,
1955-   . II. Title

HN31.M33 1988   261.8'3   C88-095108-7

Second Printing 1989

ISBN: 1-55011-055-1

©1988 by Welch Publishing Company Inc.

Welch Publishing Company Inc.
960 The Gateway
Burlington, Ontario
L7L 5K7   Canada

Printed in Canada

Cover Photo by Ron Cole

Contents

Diane Forrest is a writer and editor working in books, magazines, television and feature films. She first interviewed Bob McClure when working on her previous book, *The Adventurers*. She has also travelled widely in the Far East.

Introduction

In some ways I guess I'm really a very shallow person. I'm not good at analysing *myself*. Sometimes, as a supposed church leader, I get roped into buzz sessions in which everyone is supposed to examine the feelings they had about a particular incident. I can't remember what my feelings were. But what I *do* remember are stories. One of my favorites is about Prime Minister Diefenbaker.

After independence it became customary in India to ask the ex-maharajahs to entertain official visitors. When the late Mr. Diefenbaker was scheduled to visit in 1959, the ex-maharajah of Kota was asked to look after him. The ex-ruler immediately contacted the Canadian High Commissioner in Delhi to ask about the prime minister's preferences in wine, women and song. The High Commissioner's office replied that since Mr. Diefenbaker's wife, Olive, would be accompanying him, no dancing girl companions need be provided. As far as wine was concerned, the prime minister was a teetotaller. And he was not particularly famed for his musical appreciation.

The only helpful suggestion was that he was fond of fishing. The fishing was good in Kota, but the equipment used was dynamite or hand grenades. One struck the fuse or pulled the pin, counted to ten, and then threw the explosive into the water. The explosion produced lots of fish. The High Commissioner discreetly suggested that for one as famous for indecision as Mr. Diefenbaker, such fishing might be too risky. However, it was agreed that a tiger hunt would be a suitable entertainment.

Tigers came out at night to lurk by the ponds and catch the other animals who came to drink. The beaters would tether a buffalo calf — not a cow calf, since it is holy — beside a pond. When the tiger approached the calf, the hunters could shoot it from a little *machan*, or platform, built in a nearby tree, using a .50-calibre double-barrelled rifle with the kick of an anti-tank weapon.

Mr. Diefenbaker was duly installed in the *machan*, where the servants served tea as the sun set. Through the jungle they could hear the sound of gongs and noisemakers as the beaters drove the tiger toward the pond. As they drew nearer, the buffalo calf tugged at the tether and bawled in panic. Then they heard the grunt of the tiger as he scented his prey. Finally, the glint of moonlight revealed the shadow at the edge of the jungle, ready to pounce on the calf. The maharajah gave Diefenbaker a faint nudge in the ribs and whispered, "Now!" Diefenbaker fired. The tiger roared and leaped back into the jungle. Diefenbaker had shot the calf. His notes simply record that he "did not make a kill."

A few months after this incident I was in Kota to inaugurate a new Rotary Club. Since the members knew I was a Canadian, they all joked that I must not "do a Diefenbaker." That became the phrase in the Hindi language for making a good speech on the wrong subject.

Some stories are just fun, like that one. But others, I think, have an important message. As I travel, I may see a certain incident, and it will recur to me at night when I'm trying to sleep. I'll then realize that even though it may have been a very small event, it had significance.

Because of my age and the places I've travelled, many of those incidents are unique, and I feel I have a responsibility to share them. I realize that I am among the few survivors of a very interesting period in history, and therefore I notice changes that other people don't even realize are happening. I know things about China, for example, that very few people are aware of because so few of my generation are still living.

Canadian society has also changed a great deal. Some of the changes have been for the good, of course. I think I ought to talk about those and reinforce them. Some of the changes have not been for the good, and I think we can recognize that by looking at how other societies deal with the same situations.

Because I have a different perspective on these issues, I feel I have a responsibility to talk about them, particularly with young people. I try to get to a high school every week and sit down with about forty students in a relaxed setting and say, "What do you as Canadians have to learn from the student from another country? Today he's learning a lot about you, and you'd better learn something about him, because inevitably we are coming closer all the time." It intrigues me that there are literally thousands of students and other visitors coming here from foreign cultures, looking at our society with complete objectivity. They don't know why a certain custom or problem exists so they ask important and sometimes embarrassing questions. "Why can't a person walk safely around the city at night?" "Why do you have people of 'no fixed address'? Everybody in our country has a home." "Why are so many of your older people in institutions?" "Why do you have so many single teenaged mothers when you have all the methods of birth control available?"

The students I speak with respond very well. Some of them write back to me, even years later, and say the discussion made an impression on them. I get a kick out of that, and it fuels me for the next run. However, like Diefenbaker,

I've been known to shoot the buffalo calf — I've shot a lot of them. But I hope for your sake this book isn't one of those times.

1

An Interdependent World

One day a few years ago I was speaking at a high-school career day along with a very successful businessman. He was telling the students how proud he was to be a "self-made man" who valued his "independence."

While the students fidgetted in their seats, he went on to explain that one of the reasons he was "self-made" was that he had worked his way through college. I'd worked my way through college, too, but I had had a slide rule at that time and knew that for every dollar I had put into my education, the Ontario taxpayer had put in six. Today that figure is more like ten dollars for every one the student contributes. Using that guideline, this businessman was perhaps only about nine percent self-made.

As he went on to talk about his "independence," I noticed that he was wearing a pair of Italian shoes, a French necktie, a Swiss watch, a suit of Australian wool woven in Japan and tailored in Hong Kong and a Korean-made shirt. He had probably started his morning with a glass of juice made from Caribbean oranges and a cup of coffee from Brazil. He drove to the school in a German-made Mercedes, with tires of Malaysian rubber, powered by Persian Gulf gasoline. So much for his independence. As we walked out of the assembly, one of the students said to me, "That old so-and-so couldn't have knitted himself a diaper!"

In our world today, no one can be completely independent. When the American astronauts took their picture of the earth, that picture was seen by more people than any other visual image down through the ages. But even more important, that picture brought the same thoughts to everyone who saw it — the rice farmer in Thailand, the Mongolian nomad, the financier going to his office on Wall Street: we're all on this earth together; it's all we've got; let's make the most of it.

To put it another way, we're like passengers on a giant ocean liner. Some of us are travelling first-class, some are travelling second-class, and a whole lot of folk are crowded together on the third-class deck. Every once in a while one of us in the first-class looks down to the lower decks and says, "You know, I think third-class is sinking. Isn't that too bad?" What we don't realize is that if third-class sinks, we're certainly going to get our feet wet, and pretty soon we'll be swimming for our lives.

I'm not afraid of this interdependence — as long as we recognize how much we depend on other people and how much they depend on us. When we forget that, however, the results can be disastrous.

In the 1950s, when I was stationed in India, there was a very serious famine. The monsoons had failed, creating a two-year drought. Finally, in 1958, a front-page story in the Bombay papers read: Bulk tanker with Canadian wheat arrives!

I was at the harbor in Bombay, clearing some radium and an Indian friend — a chemical engineer trained at McGill — said, "Let's go see it." We stood there and watched this

40,000-ton tanker of Canadian wheat coming into a hungry country. I felt pretty good about being a Canadian at that moment! Indian workers unloaded the wheat, packed it carefully into bags, and since it was the rainy season, they covered it with tarpaulins so that not a grain would be spoiled.

Several more shipments arrived over the next few weeks, and then, suddenly, they stopped. Everyone wondered what had happened. According to the treaty with Canada, there was still more wheat to come, but for about six weeks, nothing arrived. Finally, the shipments started again. Later we heard that there had been a longshoremen's strike in Vancouver. The workers settled for an increase of about twenty-one cents an hour, and some improvements in benefits and working conditions. It's been estimated that during that strike, 20,000 Indian children died.

Today that tragedy couldn't happen; India is more or less self-sufficient in food. However, there are just as many other ways in which we rely on each other. Third World countries are still depending on Western nations for help, and in that kind of world, Canada has a special role to play.

Because I've lived abroad most of my life, I've tended to look at Canada from a distance, and I can see the special advantages we've had. First of all, Canada has never been devastated by an international war — and that's not true of many countries in the past eighty years. Also, we've never suffered the internal conflicts other countries have had. Those of us who worked through the wars in China and through the Second World War used to say that an international war smashes the furniture, but a civil war tears the family apart. A civil war breaks and shatters a country, and the scars last for a hundred years or more. We can see that even in America, where some of the problems caused by the Civil War of the 1860s have not yet been overcome. In Chi-

na, the upper middle class was liquidated and entire
families were wiped out. It's estimated that about forty million people were wiped out between 1945 and 1949. Nothing
like that has ever happened in Canada.

We've also been spared dictatorship. We may have had
some funny people in Ottawa now and then with strange
ideas about how to run the country, but we've never had an
actual dictator. And we've never lived in a police state. We
don't understand what it means to meet a friend and not be
able to talk freely to him or her. I remember passing
through Europe in the Thirties and stopping in Hamburg to
see some younger friends I had there. This was at the height
of one of Hitler's purges. In order to have a good talk in freedom we had to take a little fourteen-foot dinghy out into the
middle of a lake.

When it comes to dealing with people in the Third World
countries, we have a special position as Canadians. This
was summed up by a student in Calgary who said to me,
"Isn't it interesting that nobody's lying awake in Siberia tonight in case the Canadian navy makes a landing on their
coast." The very idea sounds ridiculous. Yet at this very moment, in the Mediterranean, in the Persian Gulf, all along
the Atlantic coast, from Africa right up to Spitsbergen, the
radar stations are going, the airplanes are being readied,
someone's ready to push the red button. In the middle of all
this international paranoia, nobody's afraid of Canada.
What a marvellous thing that is, and what a privileged position it gives us!

When we sign a treaty with another country, nobody sus-
pects that there is a fine-print clause about landing fields for
spy planes, docking facilities for nuclear submarines, stock-
piles of atomic weapons or secret radio-listening stations.
Our journalists and missionaries and fact-finding tours can
go places where Americans and even Britons cannot go.
Our companies are welcome where other foreign firms are

not. If American businesses go in, people suspect them of trying to spread American influence or spy for the CIA. The British may be trying to regain economically what they lost politically when the Empire died.

But Canada has never had any colonies, and we don't want any. We've never ruled anyone but ourselves. Colonialism did terrible things to the minds of the people who did the ruling. Little fellows with no great character or talent were put in charge and given tremendous power. But Canada is free from that. There are very few countries in the world who are in this favorable position — the Scandinavian countries, Finland, Switzerland, Australia, New Zealand and Canada — and we are the largest in economic and industrial terms.

We're also a senior member of that sentimental group called the Commonwealth. It may not mean very much to us, but it means a lot to others, such as India, Malaysia, Singapore, Uganda and Kenya. To them, Canada is the "big sister" who made it.

I'll always remember the thrill I got on my first day in India. I went by myself to a Rotary Club meeting, and there was nobody to introduce me to these people with a different language, different religion, different culture. One man in particular was very nationalistic. He had on his Congress uniform — his Congress hat, his Congress cloak, his *dhoti*, those trousers that are like a cross between a diaper and a spinnaker jib (cool in summer but dangerous in a high wind!). Manohar Nagpal was a Congressman to the core and had no reason to love white men. As we were going out the door, this stranger put his arm around my shoulders and said, "Isn't it wonderful? We're all members of the Commonwealth." Manohar, who was a disciple of Gandhi, later became my best friend and was a tremendous influence on my thinking.

When my wife Amy and I were leaving India in 1967 after

thirteen years there, Manohar came to say goodbye. He
shook hands with me and said, "Bob, you're going back to
Canada for good. I shall be remaining in India. We shall
probably never see each other again. There is only one message I will ask you to take as we depart. When you get back
to Canada, ask the people there if they are sure that it was
their ancestors who put the gold in the rocks of Canada."
You see, Manohar was a Hindu, and he had some peculiar
ideas. He thought maybe God had put the gold there.

In fact, the word for "natural resources" in several languages is "God's gifts." To many Third World people, min-
erals, forests and even water power do not belong to
countries or corporations; they are just the trustees. What
Manohar was trying to tell us is that with all the privileges of
our prosperity and our international position come obligations. Our sister countries in the Third World look to us for
help in all fields of development — agriculture, education,
industry and health work.

Already we've had some great successes in agriculture.
But what we have to remember is not to try to do things our
way. If we send someone who automatically tries to farm the
way we do in Canada, his work may be completely out of
step with what the people in that country need. What developing countries want is someone trained in agriculture who
can recognize their problems and use Canadian experience
and know-how to solve them. A good example is triticale, a
rye-wheat cross that was developed by scientists from many
Third World countries working with researchers at the University of Manitoba. Because it needs very little rainfall,
triticale has opened up cereal production in dry parts of the
world where, before, nothing at all would grow.

Another area in which Canada can help is in literacy —
in fact, we're learning a lot in our own country about the
problem of adult literacy, lessons that can be applied to

Third World countries. I saw what a tremendous difference literacy can make in a country when I was in China in the 1920s and 1930s. Although there were many attempts at reform in the early part of the century, the spirit of revolution never penetrated deeply in China until after the First World War. Forty thousand coolies went off to serve in that war, and when they left, scarcely a single one could read. But when they came back, they were literate. That was because of Jimmy Yen, a sociologist with the YMCA, and his young assistant, Chou En Lai. Jimmy Yen developed and taught the coolies a basic language of 800 words. When they came back, those men became the foundation of a rural reconstruction movement in China. All the newspapers, textbooks, the pamphlets on co-operative societies and health care began to be written in that basic language. For the first time there was a tremendous effort to promote change among the common people.

We tend to forget how important education is. The development of an entire country will lag behind until literacy catches up. Canadians can help by experimenting, simplifying local languages, perhaps helping to create alphabets and write dictionaries.

Another way we can help is through joint enterprises in business. Developing countries can produce as well or better than we can if Western countries will help with seed money and training. In China I saw oil-drilling crews who were trained on the east coast of Canada and are now working on the rigs on the China Sea. The Chinese have developed a tractor based on the type originally manufactured by Caterpillar many years ago, and they are now turning out ninety tractors a shift, two shifts a day.

By working together to solve these kinds of problems, we can accomplish far more in world development and peace than we can through any military means. The people of the

Third World are looking to Canada for this kind of help, and I'd like to think that Canada can rise to the occasion.

However, anyone who thinks of international development as the wise and wealthy nations of the West bestowing the benefits of their superior technology and understanding on an impoverished world has missed the point. The secret of getting along in this world, I believe, is to give and take. We may not feel we "depend" on the Third World for anything, but, as Canadians, we need to ask ourselves not only what we have to offer, but what other countries can offer us.

Our country is relatively young, and there are many things we can learn from these older cultures. For example, Canada, like much of the Western world, is becoming a land of high-density living. But this lifestyle is new to us, and we're having trouble adapting to it.

We can learn something from the Iban of Borneo who've been living in close quarters for more than six centuries. These tribal people live in longhouses, with communal porches stretching in front and a private sleeping room and kitchen for each family behind. It's really an apartment building laid on its side, raised above the ground on stilts to keep it safe from snakes and flooding rivers. Anywhere from eighteen to fifty-five families may live in these homes that stretch along the river. The Iban have learned long ago which corners need to be rubbed off in order to have harmonious living!

Even though they were once famous as head-hunters and pirates, the Iban have developed a social system based on non-violence and mutual trust and support. In the two-and-a-half years I worked with them, I never saw a violent quarrel or heard one man cursing another. I never even heard an argument between a customer and a shopkeeper. And I never had to repair an injury caused by a fight. Yet every boy and girl, when he or she reaches the age of ten, is given a long, razor-sharp machete, or *parang*, which never leaves the Iban's side. This long knife is used for slashing through jungle trails, cutting wood for the fire or killing snakes and wild animals. At least five times a week I had to sew up accidental cuts, but I never saw one cut made in anger. The Iban have learned that when you carry in your hand the power to kill, you can't afford to have temper tantrums. Complete non-violence is the only way to survive.

The other thing we can learn from this society is their lack of covetousness. Nothing is stolen and nobody has to lock up anything because the Iban don't think of wanting someone else's possessions. Once I left my camera on one of the river boats, a long motor launch that can carry 100 passengers. I thought my camera was gone for good, but three days later a man, dressed only in the briefest of briefs but with the most marvellous tattoos all over his body, showed up with my camera. He had travelled ninety miles to find me. He refused to take any reward; it was mine, so of course he had brought it back to me. But he did have one favor to ask me. "Doc, if I want to take a picture some time, let me borrow this thing, will you? And Doc, if there's ever anything of mine you need, feel quite free to borrow it."

The lesson is to be happy with what you have and not to hanker after something someone else has that you don't need, because you know that if you do need it some day, the other person will lend it to you. The Iban have learned how to respect and support each other. How different that is from our own society, where we have a multi-million-dollar advertising industry designed mainly to make us covet what other people have.

We can also learn how to live together from China and its fantastic community organization. There, everyone is very much "his brother's keeper." Everyone feels that they "belong" to the community. As a result, even though their cities are huge, the Chinese have been able to minimize the problems of crime, juvenile delinquency and homelessness.

The Chinese started a system of community organization as early as the 1930s and developed it through the Second World War. This is how it works. Every ten households elects a leader; ten leaders then elect an elder; ten elders elect an alderman; and so on. If you have guests coming to stay overnight, for example, mention to your leader that "the Smiths are arriving from Winnipeg by train this afternoon. They're coming to visit and do some shopping. They will be here for a week and will be returning home by train on Sunday night." That way your neighbors know who the strangers are going in and out of your house. Otherwise, they will investigate. The neighbors aren't prying into your privacy; they just want to be sure that you and the community are safe.

The community is also responsible for keeping an eye on the behavior of its members. When I returned to China in 1981, I noticed the enormous number of bicycles. If you were to visit a city of some six million people, there would probably be more than three million bicycles. Outside of a school office or factory there are rows and rows of bikes, all looking remarkably alike. "Why don't they get stolen?" I asked the leader of a commune I was visiting. He explained that it did happen now and then that some ignorant boy might steal a bike. But what can he do with it? If Charlie takes it home, the neighbors ask, "Where did you get the bike? How much did you pay for it? Where did you get the money? Have you registered it?" When it becomes clear that Charlie stole the bike, the Community appoints two elders to go with him and take the bike back to the place from which he stole it. They put on it a note of apology and Charlie's address. Charlie has learned his lesson. The police are not involved. There's no arrest, no criminal record.

Because of this sense of communal responsibility, there's no such thing as a person "of no fixed address" in China. My Chinese friends are shocked when they visit Toronto and see the street people who have no homes and no one to care for them. In China, every institution is responsible for housing its employees. If you are employed by a school, for example, the school has to house you along with every single employee, right down to the lady who works in the cafeteria. The same applies to a factory, a hospital, and so on. And now you are even entitled to housing when you retire. The same is true of education: every institution is responsible for educating the children of its workers. In our Western companies, we often don't give a hoot what the worker does when he or she isn't actually working on the premises.

The Chinese are even beginning to apply this principle of mutual responsibility in their prisons. It's expensive to keep someone in prison for twenty years for a serious crime. In Canada, it costs us $40,000 a year, yet we don't do a very good job of reforming people. Often, when we let a prisoner out on parole, he just goes out and does the same crime all over again — except he probably does it better because of the tips he picked up in prison. But in one experiment in China, it's the other prisoners who decide when a person is truly reformed and should be released. Bill is not merely remorseful and soggy and telling a hard-luck story; he really has learned to control his temper and stop drinking. So Bill is let out. But, if he commits a crime again, not only will he be put back in prison, but all the prisoners who recommended that he be released will have their sentences extended by six months or more. The prisoner who lets his buddies down is not only back in prison but he's in big trouble!

Another major social problem in the West is divorce. Here also we can learn from other cultures. We don't seem to be able to dissolve a marriage that isn't working without a great deal of animosity and trauma for the kids. It's all very different from my first exposure to divorce Muslim-style.

When I was stationed in Gaza in the early 1950s, the local doctor had me over for dinner every second Sunday. Dr. Abu Gazallah had a wonderful home life, with four delightful children and an attractive wife who was also a marvellous cook. But one day I learned to my surprise that she was not his first wife. "When I was sixteen years old," he explained, "I was an excellent student and wanted to go to medical school, but we had no money. My parents solved the problem very nicely by marrying me to a forty-year-old Iranian widow who was quite rich. It was an ideal marriage. I had what she wanted; she had what I needed.

"Everything was very happy. We moved to Beirut, where I went to medical college. We didn't live in the dormitory. We had a nice apartment down by the beach. The other boys were worried about money and books and girlfriends. We bought all the medical books, and I had my own microscope. With no worries, naturally I graduated at the top of my class, and then I decided to take a post-graduate course in tropical medicine in London. Again, while the other boys were broke and lonely and suffering from indigestion from the local food, I stood at the top of my class. Then we returned to Gaza, and I thought to myself, 'I don't want to set up practice married to an old hag.' So I divorced her."

I was shocked. "Dr. Abu Gazallah, you cad!" I said. "How can you divorce a woman just like that?"

"Oh, it's no trouble at all," he explained. "You just 'alas' her — wipe your hands of her three times. It was all very friendly."

"But you'd ruined her," I protested.

"Oh, no. She married another medical student three months later. She kept the books and the microscope. And I married my present wife."

"Would you ever divorce her?" I asked.

"Never. First of all, she's the mother of my children. And besides that, she comes from a very powerful family. Her brother has been mayor of Gaza for eight years. The idea of divorce never crosses my mind." And with a smile he drew his hand across his throat in a slitting motion.

I'm not sure I'd recommend the same procedure for everyone, but it was certainly divorce without trauma. He had a wonderful home, was very loyal to his second wife, and he was still on friendly terms with his first wife. His children referred to her as their "first mother," even though there was no blood relationship.

The Arabs in Gaza had such a sensible attitude to marriage. All the marriages were arranged, and before the wedding a whole contract was worked out concerning what each family owed the other and how things would be arranged if there was a divorce. That contract was approved by all the important members of the two families. Most of the marriages were happy, but if they weren't, they were very easily dissolved. Today, in many parts of the Arab world, the woman can also "alas" the husband. She doesn't have to wait until she's been repeatedly beaten up. She just stands up in front of witnesses, renounces the marriage and goes back to her family. There's nothing traumatic about it, and there's nothing to prevent her from getting married again in a few months. There's no social stigma. It's divorce without trauma, and yet divorce is not any more common in those societies than in our own.

What works in a foreign culture may not work in Canada. The Iban and the Chinese and the Arabs haven't created a paradise. We don't have to *adopt* their solutions outright. But we can at least look at these cultures and see if there's something we can learn from them, something we can *adapt* to our own society. We should be doing that in our schools and universities. It *is* possible to change. I've seen it in China, where Chairman Mao said, "Any social change can be made in one generation." We think of a generation as being thirty-three years, but he meant one generation of high-school students, which is five years.

I've seen dramatic change in Singapore, that vigorously anti-Communist country, which applied Mao's rule to change its society. At the end of World War II, Singapore was without a doubt one of the dirtiest cities on earth. It was the largest and busiest ocean port in the world, but it had been badly damaged by the war. It had the largest red-light area in the world, gambling dens galore and was the heart of the illegal drug trade, with both licensed and unlicensed opium dens. The streets were filthy. Open sewer ditches one foot wide and up to three feet deep ran along each side, and pedestrians ran the risk of being hit by garbage from the windows above.

Prime Minister Lee Kwan-Yew went to the students in the secondary schools and asked them what should be done to create the kind of city they would like to live in. They told him: "Cover the sewers, clean up the red-light area, regulate gambling and control the drugs." He replied, "Yes, but only with your help. If I do all of these things, will you take responsibility for the litter problem?"

From then on it was the students who looked after the litter. If you dropped a cigarette butt on a street in Singapore, no policeman said anything. It was the student who came over, pointed out the butt and the litter tin on every second lamppost and politely showed you how to put your litter in the can. The police didn't have to lift a finger. Eventually there was not so much as a burnt match or a soft-drink straw on the sidewalks of that city of two million people. It took nearly ten years, but today Singapore is one of the cleanest cities in the world and has one of the highest living standards in Asia.

When some nursing friends came to visit me from Singapore, they stared at the gum wrappers, the empty Coke tins and crumpled newspapers on the Toronto subway. Then they said to me quietly, in Chinese, so that no one would be offended, "Do Canadians really like to live like pigs?" In Singapore there's a $50, on-the-spot fine for littering, and it's enforced.

That kind of determination is just one of many lessons we can learn from the "underdeveloped" world, one of the qualities we might want to adapt to our own situation, because in an interdependent world, we need to help each other, listen to each other and learn from each other — or else, we're all in big trouble.

2

Hope and Terror

We live in a revolutionary age. Aside from political revolutions, there are revolutions in business, in industry, in communications, in medicine. But it seems to me that there is one revolution that is more universal and perhaps even more important than all of these changes. That is the revolution of rising expectations.

A few years ago I was riding on a crowded passenger train in central India. I always travelled third-class because the two ends of the train arrive at approximately the same time anyway, and you meet more people in third-class, whether you like it or not. I was looking at a magazine with glossy pictures, and when I finished it, I put it on the seat beside me. A young Hindu boy of thirteen or fourteen asked permission to look at it. I doubt if he could read any of it, but he looked it over with great attention. When he was finished, he passed it on to his father, then someone else took it.

By the time the journey was over, the magazine had been looked at by nearly 100 people. When it came back, the young boy picked it up again and turned to an ad that showed a shiny new car on a beautifully paved road, beside a clean sidewalk. Well-dressed people walked in front of shop windows packed with clothing, shoes and jewelry. The value of the items in that picture was probably greater than what all of those 100 people would make in their entire lives. The young boy gave his father a nudge, pointed to the picture and said, "A bit of that wouldn't be too bad, would it, Dad?"

That is the propaganda of rising expectations. None of those people could afford what was in that picture, but they knew that in other parts of the world, other people had these things — and they couldn't think of a good reason why they shouldn't have them too.

If you travel abroad today, you may not be aware of this change in attitude. People in the Third World often hide it because they don't want to offend you and they *do* want your American Express cheques. But if you understand their language and get into their homes, you can see the change.

Thirty years ago, when disaster struck a family — famine, for example — the Hindu might lift his eyes to heaven and say, "That is my *karma*, that is my fate. I must accept it." A Chinese would look at all the different alternatives, and if he found nothing, he would shrug his shoulders and say, "*Mei yu fa tze*. There's nothing I can do." The Muslim explanation of anything bad that came to him used to be "*Min Allah*. It is from Allah. I must accept it." But that response is less and less likely today. More likely the Hindu or the Chinese or the Muslim has heard that there is food in other lands, that they can even afford to waste it in some places, and so he says to himself, "I must try to get a share of that food for my wife and kids who are starving."

I saw the same spirit again in a camp for boat people, in Kowloon in Hong Kong. The refugees there were on their way to Canada, perhaps to the States, maybe to one of the

European countries — anywhere, just so that they could get a little land and settle down. It was a camp of 10,000, in a city where there were 30,000 declared refugees — who knows how many undeclared refugees there were. In the group I spoke with, everyone had been there at least three years; some had been there for five years. They were billeted in a huge Quonset hut along with 300 other people. The accommodation for each family was five feet wide, five feet high and eight feet long. They cooked outside the door on a little stove.

The refugees looked around before they spoke, to see that none of the supervisors could hear. "We've been here such a long time," they said. "We were born at the wrong time, in the wrong place. We're out of luck and we know it." And then they lifted their clenched fists and they said, "But by God we are ready to die if necessary to see that our kids have a better chance in a better world." They said it that way because it wasn't going to *be* a better world if it didn't include a better chance for their kids. And they weren't going to let *you* build a better world if it didn't take their kids into account. Those refugees knew their lives might not improve, but they were ready to sacrifice themselves for the next generation. I think that's such a positive sign, if we can respond to it.

Back in Toronto I saw the results of that determination. One day in 1984 I saw four boys at the Bloor-Yonge subway station. One of them had a little map. I stepped up and asked them if I could help them. They were very surprised that I spoke to them in Chinese. "We're trying to get to Woodbine station," they told me. I explained to the boys that I had worked in China and that I had seen their refugee camps in Hong Kong. They were delighted to meet someone who understood their situation, so we went all the way to the eastern end of the subway line then back again while they told me their story.

They were from two middle-class families who had been on the wrong side in the Vietnam War. When the Communists took over, the parents knew there was little future for them there, so they sold everything they had — everything in the shop, the shop itself, their clothes — and they put the boys in a leaky boat with about forty other people. They had to pay in gold for the trip, around $3,000 for each boy. They told the boys, "Someday, if you're very fortunate, you might get to Canada. If you do, don't forget us." Then the parents turned and went home to die.

Despite all the odds, the boys had survived, and only the other day they had received a letter through one of the relief organizations and discovered that their folks were still alive. They told me, "We're going to learn to speak English. We'll work at anything, we don't care what it is, and go to school part-time. But we'll get the money and we'll bring our parents home."

It was hope that led those parents to invest $3,000 in each of those kids, and it was hope that gave the kids the courage to keep going. Although I never saw them again, I'm quite sure that eventually they did bring their parents to Canada.

Millions around the world are surviving on that kind of hope, and it's a new, more militant kind of hope. It's not just a passive idea that maybe things will get better some day but a powerful hope for a better world, for a new life.

What happens, though, when that hope is repressed? What happens when people start to think that they're never going to get a fair deal? Where does all the energy for positive change go?

There's a balance between militancy and hope, as if they were sitting at either end of a teeter-totter. If there is a tremendous amount of vigorous hope, then there is almost no militancy at all. But as change is deferred and people give

up hope, the hope rises up and becomes lighter and lighter
and the militancy becomes greater. And finally, when people think there is no hope left, terrorism emerges. That is an
inevitable result.

I saw the beginnings of that balance between hope and
terror operating in the 1950s, when I was working in Gaza.
Instead of just accepting their fate, people were beginning to
ask why they were in that situation. Most of the older
Palestinian refugees would say, "Our wretched condition
here is from Allah." But I began to see some of the younger
people muttering, "That's not so. There's some other answer." You could just see it building up.

I went to Tripoli in Jordan in 1970 to see the PLO training
camp. None of the young people there were over twenty-five,
and many of them were just seventeen or eighteen. They
were the cream of the crop, but they were bitter, and they
knew they were going to die. The trainer would even tell
them the statistics: "Once you get into the field with the
PLO, you'll be lucky to survive two years." It was a mass
kamikaze parade. Two of the young men I met there I had
delivered as babies in Gaza, and I suppose they are now
long dead. Sadly, those boys and girls had reached the point
where they didn't look for hope because they didn't believe
that hope was there.

I saw that equation whenever I worked in a country that
had a terrorist movement. Terrorists who were captured
would often be brought into the hospital. Some of them
were the second generation of displaced people; in the Middle East now they are the third generation. In many parts of
the world children are being brought up in households
where hatred is served up at every single meal. The Sikhs
must hate the Hindus. The Catholics hate the Protestants.
The Shiites hate the Sunnis. And so on. Eventually the child
comes to feel, "Why not bump off somebody from the other

side?" They see nothing good about the person they want to kill, and there's a fifty-fifty chance they won't get caught. Even if they do get caught, they have no hope in life anyway.

The result is that as fatalistic hope passes out, militant hope comes in, and that's when we face this terrible equation: unless the hope gets some results, there will be an increase in militancy, and when the hope is gone, all that is left is militancy or terrorism.

Suddenly, we ourselves are threatened. How do we try to protect ourselves against terrorism? By hiring more guards. By having better airport security. By creating special fighting units to deal with terrorists. We call this anti-terrorism, and it's one of the craziest ideas in the world. We have to realize that we are never going to be able to beat the terrorists because they have one key advantage. Because his hope is gone, the terrorist is not afraid to die. Death is the ultimate threat. "If you don't do what I want you to do, you'll die." But if the terrorist isn't afraid of death, then you're completely powerless! This is the great thing that separates him from us. We're afraid to die. We want to live on. But he just wants to swap one life for another. One-for-one, that's a pretty good bargain. If he can make it five-for-one, that's even better.

And so violence creeps in and our modern civilization has no way to defend itself. We can't live inside a glass bubble. Our society can't function that way. If someone really wants to murder somebody and is not afraid to die, he can do it. There was an incident recently in which a man wanted to kill his boss, so he wrecked a plane, taking forty-three other lives with him. There's nothing society can do. We cannot protect ourselves against random violence.

The situation is even worse today because of the type and scale of weapons and explosives now available. There was a little terrorism in the jungle in Borneo when I was there.

The guerrillas came from the Indonesian side, we presumed, across the mountainous spine of Borneo. When the army captured some of these people's weapons, they turned out to be the latest models. I remember seeing one place where the people had left the food in their bowls and the fire still burning and their equipment scattered all around.Their transmitter was the latest compact model, running on storage batteries. Among their weapons was one that had been submitted in a bid to rearm the Canadian forces. Canada decided instead to take the model that was about $50 cheaper, but that little terrorist group had the model that Canada turned down as being too expensive. I thought it was ironic that eventually the forces facing the terrorists would probably have the cheaper weapons; the terrorists would have the deluxe models.

This belief that we can outwit terrorism always reminds me of the monkey we used to keep on the front porch of our home in North Toronto. We tried to keep that monkey tied up, but he could get away from almost anything you could put on him. We tried a padlock, and he even got away from that. My father used to enjoy watching him and he told me, "You know, Bob, you can't win at that game, because he has nothing else to do. And we *do* have something else to do. The monkey has almost as good a brain as we have and he can spend all his time figuring out how to get loose. So he's always going to get away."

Like our monkey, the terrorist has nothing else to do. He is dedicated to destruction while we're distracted by all the other aspects of running our society. We have to realize that we can never win, and we also have to realize that there is no nation so antiseptic that it's proof against terrorism.

I always liken our present methods of dealing with terrorism to the pre-antibiotic days in medicine. It's as if we were trying to treat typhoid by giving the patient aspirin to bring down the temperature or curing TB by giving cough medicine to stop the cough. By trying to stop bombings and plane hijackings, we're only dealing with the symptoms.

We know that the answer is something far more fundamental than that. We had to remove the *cause* of the typhoid and remove the *cause* of the TB. In the same way we'll have to remove the *causes* of terrorism, and we'll have to do it on an international scale. We have to get at the roots of terrorism. The answer is to see that justice is done and that people do not have cause for this resentment that drives them to violence. We must remove the cause of the violence by giving the terrorist back his hope. We have to say, "You have struggled for something, and now we're going to pay attention to it." And if we're honest, we'll also have to say that we are paying attention because terrorism called it to our attention.

People say, "How you do reestablish that hope? That alone is an impossible task." I don't believe it's impossible. You can do it if you have the right spirit, but it will take a long time and a lot of patience and imagination and effort. The longer we leave it, the more difficult it will be.

People do not forget injustice or a long-standing feud easily, but it is possible. You only have to look around at the countries that were bitter enemies during the Second World War and are now allies.

I've seen that kind of reconciliation happen on a personal level. In the fall of 1945 our ambulance unit had shared space with a group of about 400 Japanese. V-J Day was in August, but there was nobody there to accept their surrender until Christmas. During that time they were quite helpful to us, sharing their supplies and showing us where to find lumber. Finally they were told that they could surrender, but they would have to move themselves down to Hankow, using their little Chevrolet truck and hauling about eight open cars behind it. They got to Hankow, where there were already 2,500 Japanese, and discovered that the Chinese had made no provision to feed them. The Chinese chucked them behind barbed wire and didn't give them any food.

One day, a New Zealander from our ambulance unit happened to be in Hankow and recognized them. He remembered what a help they'd been to us and was worried that they would starve to death. So he went down to the American navy and explained the situation. The navy moved in and fed the Japanese rations and accelerated their evacuation so that the whole bunch of them were on their way to Japan in two weeks.

That fellow has been invited to Japan three or four times by those soldiers, and he's an honorary member of the war veteran's association in Japan. It shows how much can be done if you really work at patching up a war. Consequently, though I can understand and sympathize with the people who keep talking about the Holocaust, I'm not sure that studying it so much is very healthy. I've never had my family murdered, I've never been in their position, and I don't know how I would react if I had. But I just don't think that constantly dwelling on the past is a good solution.

All of my friends were murdered in China, but I feel no animosity towards the governments that did it. I feel my friends just got caught up in war, which is a terrible machine. It minces people up, regardless of color, race, creed or anything else. It's shocking, but that's war, and let's look to the future instead of regurgitating the past. I don't think it's disloyal to the memory of Loving Lotus, my nurse, or any of the boys I trained. I name them over sometimes and look at old pictures, realizing once again that they were all wiped out, mostly by the Japanese, perhaps some by the Communists. It was a no-win situation.

Our job, however, is not to think bitterly about the past or to encourage other people to do that. Our job is to reestablish hope in thousands of people and convert them from a dangerous despair. Even if it takes ten or twenty or thirty years to do it, let's get started. It may be an expensive proposition, but it's cheaper than losing your life.

This doesn't mean we have to bring everybody to Canada as refugees. Often we can help them to change things in their own country. With quiet diplomacy we can pressure governments to make life better for their people. Foreign-aid projects needn't be expensive. In fact, often the most effective ones are the cheapest, and even the largest projects cost only a few million — half the cost of a fighter plane, for example, and we crash a few of those every year.

We have to get our priorities straight because this new spirit of militant hope in the world is not something that will go away if we ignore it. We're dealing with one of those great tides of history that we all too often miss.

When a news reporter or a camera crew go to another country, they may only be there for a week. They want something that's going to shake up the folks back home. What we don't realize is that over the years we have seen all the things that shake up the folks back home, and sometimes that's the *only* thing we see. It's as if we were standing on the shore of an ocean, seeing only the pounding of the waves on the rocks — the froth, the foam, the spray, while the tide slowly rises. Just as quietly as happens in nature, there are the tides of things coming. In international relations, the waves so often disturb us, but we don't pay attention to the tide. And it is the tide that is so important.

The British didn't see the tide of Gandhi. They saw the waves of the massacre in Amritsar, the riots and boycotts, but they didn't see the great tide of nationalism that was coming and would eventually sweep them away. In China, in the same way, very few people realized what a powerful force was behind the Communist movement. It was a tide of people who were fed up with the Manchu regime and fed up with what was offered as substitutes after it fell. They wanted to skip over the whole process of having a two-party system and representative government — all the political ideas that we thought were sent from heaven and carved in stone. We found those systems weren't sacred.

The Western nations have made the same mistake over and over again. In the Philippines we backed the wrong man, Marcos, because he seemed to offer us some solution to the wave problem. But people like that are going to be swamped by the tide themselves. They hold back the waves for a few years, and we think we've solved the problem. Then we can't accept the new regime that is swept in by the tide. We say, "They must be evil because they kicked out the dictator, who was a friend of ours." It doesn't matter that he was a rotten dictator. Somebody sets up a government that looks pretty good, as in Nicaragua, and we try to destroy it. We complain that it's not democratic enough.

We always assume that if others don't have the same trappings as we do, they must be a suppressed people. If a country doesn't have members of parliament elected the way we elect them, it must be a dictatorship. But a benign dictatorship can be an infinitely better government in an underdeveloped country than a fake democracy. Whatever government is set up, it must be one that the people themselves will accept. Whatever they come up with, it isn't necessarily going to be like what we have. We can't make them clones. We always ask, "Why can't they be like us?" Well, they don't want to be like us, and they don't need to be like us, and they aren't like us anyway.

That attitude reminds me of the incident in the New Testament, when disciples found someone else casting out demons and doing a pretty good job of it. They were mad as blazes that someone else was stealing their thunder and asked Jesus how they could stop him. Jesus replied, "If he can cast out demons, he can't be all bad, so let him do it." Even from the earliest times we've been allergic to seeing anyone do our job a little better than we can.

We're very foolish if we just decide that these changes are evil and try to repress them. The person who does that is like old King Canute — he had a little bit of trouble with waves and tides, too, and he got flooded out. The person who stands on the beach and tries to command the sea is ridiculous.

However, I think we can *influence* the tide. We don't have to back it politically, but I think we should try to influence and at least be friendly with it. We should be emphasizing the friendship that still exists between peoples, even when their governments aren't getting along.

I believe that we cannot afford to ignore this tide of militant hope that is sweeping over the world, because although it may sound very irreligious and very unorthodox, these tides of political change come from God.

I remember after the war some of the Chinese women who had belonged to the evangelical churches seemed to realize that. They would look around and see the changes coming in — the new buildings going up, the fields becoming green again, the floods and famine ending — and say, "Wouldn't Jesus be pleased to see the changes that are happening?"

I believe that God's spirit is working through political evolution to create something better. God plants a new political idea or spirit in people's minds that, if we can respond to it, will create a better world. And those who cannot respond are doomed.

3

Family Planning and Common Sense

One time when I was on furlough, I went to visit one of my father's colleagues, a medical missionary who was now retired and living in Montreal. One of his relatives said to me, "You should really tell him about the success of your family-planning program." It was a booby trap of the first order! I went in and effused about the terrific success of our program in India — the 500 women enrolled, all the tubal ligations and vasectomies we'd done. You could just see the old missionary's blood pressure rising as got he madder and madder. Finally he bellowed, "And who made you God?" That was the end of our interview. I ran for the door and escaped before his wrath got the better of him.

I don't know how to answer his question. I can only say that in all the years I spent on family planning, I never had the feeling I was playing God. Birth control was a matter of common sense. Through contraceptives you could raise a family's standard of living, lengthen the lives of millions of women, relieve both husband and wife of anxiety — even improve their sex lives, because once the anxiety of having an unwanted child was gone, couples usually found that sex was much more fun. To me, it's amazing that contraception is still a controversial subject in the developed world, even among those whom you think would know better.

Taking a common-sense attitude to birth control is more important than ever today, for we are dealing with an epidemic of pregnancies in the Third World. Because of better health care, children who would have died in the past are now surviving and having children of their own, and that's putting a tremendous strain on families.

One case study that the Baptists did in Assam, India, described a grandfather who had owned ten acres of land, enough to make him a wealthy man. However, his farm was now divided among twenty-seven descendants. Ten acres of land divided among that many people just doesn't support anyone; somebody's going to starve. So in Third World countries, family planning isn't an optional thing.

It's true that in an ideal world, with just political systems and fair distribution of food and the earth's wealth, there would be more than enough for everyone. But until we get a little closer to that ideal world, one way people in developing countries can better their situation is by having fewer children. Yet there are still many people who don't approve of any kind of family planning. They're opposed to abortion, but they don't want people to use contraceptives either.

I can't help thinking of the film clip they used to show on television during the Ethiopian famine. A mother was sitting on the ground with a dead child at her feet, another, obviously on the verge of death, sucking at her dry breast. As she lifted her eyes to the camera, to me she was pleading, "Can't you show me some way my husband and I can have a reasonable family life and not bring any more children into this kind of world?" I'd like to ask the people who are opposed to both contraceptives and abortion how they answer that question.

I recognize that many medical people feel uncomfortable about doing abortions. Maybe if I'd practised in Canada instead of the Third World, I'd feel the same way. In an affluent society the need for abortion is usually less desperate. If Momma ends up having six children instead of only two, with good government assistance she can still raise all those children. But I spent my childhood and most of my medical career in the Third World, and there an unwanted child is going to handicap the children the family already has. Worse, in poorer countries an unwanted child is usually condemned to a life of slavery or prostitution. It would probably be better if that child had died at birth. I came to feel that I would rather do an abortion, even near term, than assist at the birth of a child who wasn't wanted. To me it's the worst obscenity that a child should be born who is doomed to be unloved for the whole of its existence. It isn't wanted by the father; it isn't wanted by the mother. It's a nuisance to the family — and it's treated that way.

I came to this conclusion quite early. In fact, I did my first abortion when I was an intern at Toronto General Hospital, getting ready to go back to China as a medical missionary. Even though abortions were illegal in Canada, I agreed to perform it because both the mother's life and the father's life would have been ruined if they'd had the baby. (The girl was studying at a Bible college and her boyfriend was a theological student.)

There was no trouble with the operation, but I nearly got caught. I'd been careful to buy the drugs I needed in a drugstore at the other end of the city, but another student was doing abortions, too, and he'd stolen a whole bottle of ergot from the hospital pharmacy. I was afraid I'd be blamed.

Getting caught was the only thing that really worried me about this case. Although I certainly didn't enjoy doing it, I never had any hang-ups about the abortion because having that baby would have been so disastrous for both parents. I don't know what happened to the woman, but the man had a very happy life — including a happy marriage.

I never found much basic opposition to abortion in the Third World, in contrast to our society. The abortions in the Third World were the dirty, "back alley" type, which often killed the mother or simply didn't end the pregnancy. In fact, even today it's estimated that 100,000 women die every year from illegal or unsafe abortions. So, when people in the Third World saw our Western-style abortion, under sanitary conditions, they were so delighted that they took to it like ducks to water. Maybe too much so, because unfortunately in recent years abortion has begun to be used as a method of family planning, especially in Japan. And I think this is a very great danger.

Once when I was visiting a family-planning clinic in Osaka, I was shocked to see a woman coming into the clinic to have her third abortion in twelve months. Later on the same trip I was visiting a clinic in Taiwan. The social worker who was showing me around told me that she had already had two abortions. Then she excused herself, saying she'd have to leave because she had to be at the abortion clinic at 3:30 to have another one, but if I came to her apartment at dinnertime, she'd have a meal ready and we could talk some more. To her, abortion was a method of family planning.

Personally, I find that morally reprehensible. I've done more than 500 abortions, but I've never felt good about a single one. The fetus is a living organism — I won't say it's a baby, but it has the potential to become one — and so abortions should only be a last resort.

Today an abortion is not much more dangerous than having a tooth drilled, and as abortion becomes safer and simpler, I see a great danger that it could become a method of birth control. It's already happening in Asia, and it could easily happen here. We adapt to abortion surprisingly quickly, and that indiscriminate use of it would lead to a callousness in society — I don't think we would be a happy people.

However, the only way to avoid the unwanted child on the one hand and the necessity for abortion on the other is better family planning and better sex education at a much younger age. It's surprising that in the so-called advanced countries sex education is so much worse than in the "primitive" countries. In the Third World the child learns very, very early. He sees the chickens, the dogs, the cats and the wild animals in sexual activities. And in crowded housing, the child knows that Mommy has a swelling in her stomach and that it's a baby. This thorough knowledge of sexual matters in a young child can be such a happy thing.

I saw a glorious example in Kapit, the town where I was stationed in Borneo. Once or twice a year we'd have a big fair in town in the main square of the place. There'd be little booths — Shell Oil would have a booth, Nestle's had a booth, Coca Cola had a booth. Everybody had a booth, so family planning had a booth, too. We had the most gruesome pictures — not life-size, but three times life-size! — of the entire reproductive system of the man and the woman. Girls in white uniforms with red crosses on their sleeves gave out all the details, plus diagrams and a load of books with colored pictures. Nothing was hidden.

I remember hearing two little boys, about nine and ten, standing at our booth. After the Red Cross lady had given her spiel, the one little fellow turned to the other and said, "Hey, you know, my mom uses the Pill." The other kid replied, "Pills ain't no good. My ma's got a loop." Here were nine- and ten-year-olds discussing the relative advantages of different contraceptives. And to think we have kids graduating from high school who still aren't sure how babies happen and how to prevent them!

It seems so hypocritical and artificial that we have deliberately hidden these facts from our young people. Certainly the sex education I got was lousy. My father was a doctor and Mother was doing welfare work with the Chinese women, but neither of them ever took me behind the barn. However, in my association with the Chinese kids, nothing was left to the imagination. Long before puberty I had all the facts of life. Don't ask me exactly where and how I got them, but I'm grateful I did. Even so, I was well into medicine before I really knew the various methods of birth control that were available.

I don't know what it is about our culture that makes us so squeamish about sex education. People seem to think that if you have sex education in the schools, it will be so arousing that you'll have copulation all over the building. I can't buy that argument. It's silly to think that kids would go wild just because they knew some of the facts of life. My theory is that if you give them the facts of life early enough, you avoid that.

In Borneo, a high-school girl could go to the school nurse and get an injection of Depro-provera to prevent pregnancy. That was perfectly routine. There wasn't any fuss. And yet there wasn't anywhere near the amount of sexual activity among the teenagers in Borneo as there is here.

Of course, if contraception and family planning are going to work, you have to be sure that the method that you're trying to introduce is acceptable to the culture. The same high-school girl in Borneo would have gotten into trouble if the nurse had put her on the Pill. Tribal people aren't accustomed to taking regular medication, and they don't have the same ideas about time that we do. The girl might have forgotten to take the Pill for four days and then taken four all at once to make up for it. The method has to work for that culture, and there has to be an educational campaign to go with it.

The best example of an effective family-planning program I saw was in India. Like most of the Asian men I encountered, the Indian husband believes he is entitled to sex every night of his married life except when his wife is menstruating, two days before the delivery of a baby, and one month after delivery. But the Indian women were determined not to have more children than they wanted, so in the early Fifties, everyone involved in community health care began to introduce contraceptives for women — IUDs, foams, diaphragms, you name it. Every gadget to prevent pregnancy was tried on the Indian woman.

The IUD was especially successful in India because once it was inserted, the woman didn't have to do anything further. One of the most popular IUDs was the Lippes loop, an S-shaped plastic rod with a little tail of purple nylon. About eighty miles down the track from our station there was an American lady who was very keen about introducing the Lippes loop to the Indian women. Because she had nursing training, she could insert the loops herself. She would give her pep talk to the women under the banyan tree, then go inside and fix up the ones she'd been able to persuade.

But the Indians were great on rumors, and the latest one was that the Lippes loop was a worm — which made sense since it looked much like the intestinal worms that many of them suffered from. The white man was putting this worm in all the Indian women, and, as a result, their children would be terribly deformed: they'd be born with white faces and big noses and blue eyes.

Consequently, when the American woman gave her little demonstration to the ladies of a particular village, they were very suspicious. She showed them a loop taken from an envelope, but they pointed at the big jar of bichloride where she kept the loops she was going to use on them. "What about those ones?" they asked. "Maybe they're different."

The American was getting impatient so, in a wonderful gesture, she fished into the jar, picked out a loop and flung it into the dust at her feet. "Look at it. It's not a worm. It's not living at all!" It was a very hot day in May, and she had forgotten that as the loop warmed up in the hot dust, the little S-curve would begin to straighten out. As the women watched, the loop started to move. They screamed and ran inside, and that was the end of that demonstration. It was another year before anyone could speak to the people of that village again about family planning. But despite these little hitches, contraceptives for women were very successful.

Then, in the early sixties, the government announced that family planning was also men's business, and male contraceptive methods were introduced. The two largest service clubs in India, the Lions and the Rotary, took a big role in convincing men to take responsibility for family planning. In a matter of two or three years, the men were starting to catch on. They didn't like condoms, so the Rotary and the Lions clubs developed the idea of a "vasectomy camp." Every night in the local villages club members would sit under a tree with a Coleman lamp and talk to the people about the population explosion. Afterwards the men would sign up.

The clubs would take over one of the schools, set up three or four operating tables, and the local doctors, who were giving up their holidays, would go at it. One of the doctors told me he did 108 vasectomies in one day. And that was only one of the four tables! No vasectomy camp would close its doors until it had done at least 1,000 vasectomies.

This all goes to show that Third World people often have a much healthier, more open attitude toward family planning. When I talk about vasectomy camps in a Rotary Club here, the men start fidgetting in their seats and asking who the speaker is next week. They don't want to hear about that! Once in an interview I happened to mention vasectomies to Gordon Sinclair. Fortunately it was a radio interview, because Gordon suddenly grabbed his pants and headed for the door, saying, "No one's going to make a soprano out of me!" Like a lot of men, he didn't have an anatomically correct idea of what a vasectomy was.

The campaign in India makes one realize how effective family-planning education can be. Thanks to Mrs. Gandhi and the service clubs, responsibility for family planning in India today is divided more equally between the sexes than in any other country.

In most countries the situation is dreadfully unfair because women have to take all the responsibility for family planning — and often for the children who result if the method doesn't work! Men aren't expected to concern themselves with birth control because of their macho image. I have a doctor friend in the Caribbean who frankly admits that he had a couple of "out" children before he was married. His wife is the mother of four children — note the way he puts it — and in the last few years he's had two more "out" children. The community accepts this behavior; he's not even criticized for it.

In Canada we all agree in theory that the man should share the responsibility for birth control and for supporting the children he produces, but it's only recently that we've put some financial teeth into this social rule. We're finally starting to track down the men who've abandoned their families and to force them to pay up. That's a big improvement, because when a man knows that he will be legally responsible for any children he might produce and that those laws will be enforced, right up to the point of garnisheeing his wages for the next twenty years, you can bet that his interest in birth-control methods is going to increase dramatically!

The other way to get men involved in birth control is through education, as happened in India. But until we get a clearer policy on sex education and overcome our ridiculous inhibitions, how are we going to introduce the idea that men are also responsible? How can we persuade young men to be involved in family planning when we're afraid to tell them how babies are made, let alone how to prevent them from being made?

Furthermore, even when Western people are well informed about birth control methods, they still have problems making up their minds. I've done more than 2,200 vasectomies and about 2,500 tubal ligations as an overseas missionary, and I never once heard anyone ask for a reversal. Yet the first thing anyone brings up here when you mention sterilization is, "What if I change my mind?" I think in simple societies people make decisions and stay with them, but in complex societies like ours, people dither right from the day they're born to the day they die.

In my overseas practice, I found that once they were offered the opportunity, most people knew exactly what they wanted from family planning, and my greatest ally was often the patient who was willing to try something new.

When we arrived in Borneo, I knew that I wanted to do family-planning work, but I didn't know how to get started. I did know from my experience that you have to begin at the top level of the local society and work down. We'd only been at our station up the river for a week when a lady came to visit us, the granddaughter of the most powerful chief among the Iban. She was tribal to the core and very proud of her heritage. While we were having tea, the princess asked me about family planning. "I have two small girls," she said, "and my husband and I don't want to have any more children. What would you recommend?" I told her that I would recommend a tubal ligation, and she was very enthusiastic. But her husband was away in New Zealand, doing post-graduate work in agriculture. "I'd need your husband's permission, wouldn't I?" I asked. "Besides, you've got two girls. Maybe you'll want a son later on?" "No, that's no problem,"she said. "You do the operation, and I'll be all fixed up by the time my husband comes home."

This was really putting my head in a noose. The other missionaries assured me though that she was a very intelligent woman and that in the Iban tradition it was the wife who decided how many children she wanted and when she wanted them. So with terrific trepidation I did the operation. I was still shaking in my boots that the husband would come back and hack off my head with a machete because I had sterilized his wife.

The day after the operation, the other Iban women began to come to me, asking if I could do the same operation for them. Because of that one woman, tubal ligations were immediately accepted among the Iban. We did at least 300 in the three years I was in Borneo, and at least 50 of those patients were personally influenced by that Iban princess to have the operation. And I still hadn't heard from the husband.

The morning of the day we were to leave Borneo, the princess came back to present us with a carved wooden shield with an inscription that read, "In grateful thanks for what you have done for our family's happiness." Apparently the husband had agreed that sterilization was a good idea. There was something else on the plaque that looked like a horned skull. It wasn't until a year later that I realized it was the ovaries and the Fallopian tubes, with the gap in the middle that I had made on each side. It was a fitting reminder of a lady who was willing to make a decision.

4

Disease:
A Winnable Battle

As a medical missionary, I had the unique opportunity of catching some of the most frightening diseases in human history. In China I caught malaria, typhus fever and relapsing fever. Good nursing brought me through safely, but many of my colleagues and patients weren't so lucky.

Although as a doctor I wasn't any more immune to disease than the victims we were treating, I was able to overcome my fears and see these epidemics as a challenge. I had complete confidence that if we put into practice all the science we knew, we could defeat the disease. But if we left one known factor out of our considerations, we would fail and it would be our own fault.

My first cholera epidemic was a horrifying sight. The mission hospital was just like a railway station, with desperately ill people everywhere. Cholera killed very quickly. A person could have a perfectly normal breakfast, get a dose of cholera in mid-morning and be dead by the early afternoon. The symptoms were cramps, severe vomiting and diarrhea — all the fluids were being completely drained from the victim's body. In the early days in China medical people just threw up their hands when a cholera case came in. We could try to stop the vomiting and diarrhea with strong opium derivatives, but the mortality rate was ninety percent.

Then, about 1932, we discovered that if we replaced the chlorine with a salt solution and could keep the patient alive for twenty-four hours, he would build up his own immunity to the disease and probably survive. Even though we had a cure, however, it was still terrifying to try to deal with that many stricken people. It wasn't always clear if the patient was alive or dead. Although we'd try to get the intravenous in as quickly as possible, often there was no pressure in the veins. So we'd put in a little local anaesthetic and cut right into the vein to get the needle in. Then we'd pump in a quart of saltwater.

The most graphic case was a man who came in about 11 A.M., a farmer who lived only half a mile from the hospital. He'd eaten a good breakfast, then gone out with his hoe to dig in his fields. Suddenly he got cramps and started to vomit. He shouted to his neighbors, "I've got the malady. Get me to the hospital!" They brought him in, but it was fifteen minutes before we got to him. I was sure he was dead, even though he wasn't stiff. Yet, I knew that a cholera victim should have rigor mortis within minutes of his death. I called to one of the assistants and told him to get some saline solution into the man, just in case. Then I went for my lunch, convinced I'd seen the last of him.

When I came back from lunch, the saline was still going, and the man was beginning to come around. By four o'clock that afternoon, he was staggering around the outpatient department, taking all the saltwater he could drink and yelling, "Where the hell's my hoe? I had a hoe when I came in here." That was the first time I realized just how dramatic a recovery from cholera could be. In the end, the new treatment was so effective that it wasn't till we got to patient number 114 that anyone died.

Our primary aim, of course, was to make sure people didn't get cholera in the first place. As soon as we realized an epidemic was starting, there were three things we had to do. We had to stop the sale of all open food, especially raw fruit, so that there would be no fly contamination. Then we had to make sure the water was safe. If the people got their water from a well, then we'd place a Boy Scout there with a pail full of emulsion of chloride of lime. He'd put a little in everyone's bucket. If anybody refused it, we'd arrange for a policeman with a pistol to be there the next day. After that, everyone co-operated. The third measure was inoculation. Fortunately, the vaccine is very easy to make, stores well and takes effect quickly and effectively. Within twelve hours of being vaccinated you are cholera-proof. (The catch is that the immunity lasts a very short time — about three months.)

The principle was the same in every disease I would deal with in China. We had to take whatever precautions we could to prevent the spread of the disease. If a vaccine was available, we would inoculate the entire population. And if there was a cure, we had to be ready to administer it. If we slipped up in any of those areas, we would be defeated. We were like generals making plans for a battle: we had to have sufficient artillery and ammunition, have our troops properly positioned, attack at a certain time of day, and so on. If we could work out all those problems, then we could win.

During the second cholera epidemic I experienced in China we organized a total vaccination campaign. That was in Guizhou which was a very backward, mountainous province with no roads, no railway and no airline. It was hard to get anywhere in that place, and there were six million people who needed to be vaccinated.

We managed to talk the French in Vietnam into sending us enough vaccine by drawing a map that showed that the cholera would reach them in a week if it wasn't stopped. We got two Chevrolet truck-loads full of vaccine, put into beer bottles rather than the usual small 40 ml bottles. We issued it to high school students and showed them how to vaccinate each other. I'm sorry to say that we used one syringe for every five people. The students were told to boil the syringe every time they used it, but I'm sure they didn't. However, they must have done a good job, because the whole epidemic was over in three or four weeks, with a very low mortality.

The third epidemic was near the end of the war. The Japanese were leaving Guilin, and there was a rumor that they had deliberately sowed cholera as they were retreating. Everyone on the Allied side was excited about this and told us to get down there and see if it was in fact a case of bacterial warfare by the Japanese. We knew better. The Japanese were more afraid of cholera among their troops than they were of the enemy, so they would never have taken that risk. By this time the civilian population was extremely well-disciplined, so we got 100-percent co-operation. We told the police what was necessary, and they passed the information on to the people. The Boy Scouts handled the vaccination. They had a map of the city and kept careful track so that nobody was missed and nobody was vaccinated twice.

Nevertheless, many people did become infected before we could get to them. There were about eight medical people from the Friends' Ambulance Unit, and we treated between 400 and 600 patients a day. Early one morning I was called to the abandoned horse stables that we were using as a hospital. There was a newborn baby there, just a few hours old, its umbilical cord still attached. "Where's the mother?" I asked the people there. "She was a refugee," they told me. "She died at about 5 o'clock, and we put her on the wagon with the rest of the corpses."

It was now about six o'clock in the morning. We rushed

out to the burial ground, where the bodies were stacked, five deep, like railway ties. Then, when there were enough bodies in the pile, they would be sprinkled with kerosene and cremated. We found the woman under another body, naked except for a few rags — but she wasn't stiff! "Get this woman out of here," I yelled. We put her on a stretcher and took her back to the hospital. We could see no sign of life — no pulse, no heartbeat, no breathing — but we cut down on her vein and filled her up with saline solution. At dusk that day, she took the baby in a basket on one end of a carrying pole and a basket with her few belongings on the other end and walked down the road, following the retreating Japanese army to whatever home she had left.

That was the last cholera epidemic I saw. Today Guilin is a major tourist attraction in China. People ask me, "Have you been to Guilin? Isn't the scenery wonderful?" But that's not what I remember about Guilin.

Cholera prevention is now so successful that in India they can have a huge religious festival that goes on for several days and there won't be a single case of cholera. Amy and I both attended the Mela festival when we were stationed at Ratlam. Up to eleven million people might attend such a festival, and the reserve police vaccinated each one as he left the train.

Typhus fever was another major problem in China. Unlike cholera, it still has no satisfactory vaccine, so its prevention and treatment required great discipline. Typhus is spread by lice, and our British and American drivers on the Burma Road often caught it from their passengers or from the inns they stayed at. Before DDT there was really no way they could keep themselves free from lice, but they did their best, boiling their underwear every night, even if it meant they had to put it on damp in the morning.

If they did get typhus fever, the men who said, "I'll keep

driving until I drop, then get help," inevitably died. But if they pulled into the nearest hospital or sent to us for help, good nursing would usually pull them through. As with cholera, the victim will build up an immunity to typhus if you can keep him alive long enough.

Typhus was also a major problem in the hospitals, especially the ones close to the front, and we had to be very down-to-earth in dealing with it. The patients all had lice, but at least you could do something for them — bathe them, change their clothes and sheets. The nurses were too busy to look after themselves, so we regularly checked their panties, doing a louse count at the end of every shift. I remember one girl who had worked from six in the morning until noon. When she finished, we asked her to change her panties. We found twenty-two animals. That was from just a half a day's work on the ward.

One of my most humiliating experiences came when we were dealing with air raid victims in 1938, trying to prevent an outbreak of typhus. There were 10,000 refugees passing through Zhengzhou every twenty-four hours on the way to western China from the war zone, and we had to find some way to delouse them. The best we could do was take their underclothes and give them a good bath while a group of women would iron the clothes to kill the lice.

A lab technician, a brilliant German representative from the League of Nations, told us he had a better idea. He would build us a delousing station. It was like an oversized chicken coop, with galvanized iron on the bottom. You lit a fire underneath, and the lice and eggs would all be destroyed in about ten minutes. Our delousing station lasted only three days. We had about forty refugees in, and while they were washing, the delousing machine caught fire! We had forty naked refugees on a cold winter afternoon, completely deloused and completely without clothing! We sent out an emergency appeal, and though the people of Zhengzhou didn't have much themselves, they managed to get together enough clothing to get those people out of the shower. We never used the delousing machine again.

Then DDT came in. It was very hush-hush — nobody was sure what it was. It was shipped over to Asia and Europe — tons and tons of it — in diluted form, four percent DDT and ninety-six percent Georgia road dust. The Allied governments wouldn't send it in pure form for fear it would fall into the hands of the enemy and they would learn the formula. The enemy was losing people from typhus just as fast as we were, and the only thing they had to kill lice was pyrethrum powder, brought over in submarines from Argentina.

DDT proved very effective at delousing, and it changed the shape of the war. It's one more example that wars are won not by bullets but by how effective you are at keeping your armies from getting cholera, typhus or other diseases.

Just as DDT made a dramatic difference in dealing with typhus, so various new drugs transformed the treatment of other diseases, such as plague. Most people associate plague with the Middle Ages, but it was a big problem in China when I was there. Bubonic plague is harbored in the rat population and spread by the fleas that live on the rats. As the rat dies, the flea needs another home. That's when it bites something else, particularly something that's on the floor. In much of China the children slept on the floor while the parents slept in a bed, so it was often the children who were infected first.

For a long time we had no treatment for the plague. The victim usually died within four or five days, and there was little we could do. It was terrifying. Even the plague vaccine didn't seem to work very well.

Then, in 1942, the sulfa drugs came in. I was dealing with

a fearful epidemic in the mountains between Burma, India and China, where the tribal people lived. A priest from the nearby mission showed me just what a difference the drugs made. In one village he visited there were forty-four children. He only had enough drugs for half of them. When we went back to that village, not one of the children who had taken the sulfa had died, and not one of the children who hadn't received any was still alive. It was the most dramatic experiment I had ever seen.

Supplies of new drugs were usually limited, and the distribution was often desperately unfair. During the war I was appointed as a consulting surgeon at the French Railway Hospital in Kunming, which gave my ambulance unit not only some urgently needed income but also access to some valuable French medicines.

The hospital catered to wealthy upper-class families, and one of the patients was the only son of a notorious black marketeer. The boy had septicemia in his leg and was going downhill fast. Nothing we tried seemed to work. I told his father that I thought our only hope was to obtain some of the new and powerful drug known to the Chinese as "bunny-she-lin" — penicillin. The only place where it was available was the U.S. Air Force base hospital, but it was reserved for American soldiers. They didn't give out penicillin even to Chinese soldiers, let alone to civilians. The father suggested I try some bribery — the sky was the limit he assured me — but I wasn't able to arrange anything.

Meanwhile, morale in China was very low. While things were improving for the Allies in the South Pacific, the situation in China was pretty grim. The Chinese feared a last great offensive by the Japanese to "finish off" China. There were even rumors that China would desert the Allies and make a separate peace with Japan. The Americans decided a gesture was needed to raise Chinese morale. They would send out Vice-President Henry A. Wallace as a gesture of solidarity with the Chinese people, and he would bring a gift for them — penicillin!

The radio and newspapers reported the progress of Vice-President Wallace as he came closer with his precious gift. Finally he landed at Chungking, at the famous airfield at the bottom of a 300-foot canyon in the Yangtze River. As his plane came in, Generalissimo Chiang Kai-Shek and his wife and the cabinet were all there to meet him. Maximum security was in force. Guards with their pistols drawn and ready surrounded the field. On the cliffs above stood snipers with their rifles in case of an assassination attempt. Among the cabinet ministers was one who was unfamiliar, wearing large dark glasses. Since there were rapid changes in the top personnel of the government at that time, everyone assumed he was a recently appointed official.

Vice-President Wallace stepped down from the plane onto the red carpet. He was greeted by Generalissimo and Mrs. Chiang and two or three cabinet ministers. The man in the dark glasses shook hands with Wallace and whispered in his ear. Wallace handed over the parcel of penicillin, and the convoy moved off to ascend the long steps to the top of the canyon.

The next day the father of our patient gave us the penicillin to treat the boy. He made a rapid recovery. No one ever figured out who the man in the dark glasses was, but penicillin was available for some time thereafter on the black market.

The new wonder drugs were not always the ideal answer, however. Our ambulance unit particularly disagreed with the U.S. Army about Atabrin, which was used to prevent malaria. Atabrin was developed for soldiers making landings on tropical islands. If you took it for fourteen days, you wouldn't get malaria no matter how many mosquitoes bit

you. But if you *kept* taking it, after thirty or sixty days you
would begin to get Atabrin poisoning. As medical people,
we weren't allowed to say that there was any danger, even
though one of our best doctors died from Atabrin poisoning.

It was the job of the commanding officer to make sure
that every American on the Burma Road took one Atabrin
at every morning parade. Of course, the soldiers cheated.
They'd keep it in their mouths and then sell it to the Chinese later. Because Atabrin was also a cure for malaria at-
tacks, there was a terrific black market in it around every
American base, and it certainly helped keep some Chinese
alive who otherwise would have died.

Today chloroquine is a much more satisfactory drug for
preventing malaria. As well, we're learning to control
mosquitoes with insecticides. But even more basic is education. In places where malaria is a problem, everyone now
knows that they should sleep under a net. Many are quite
fastidious about it, because they know that if you don't sleep
under a net, you'll get sick. It's surprising how quickly this
practice catches on. When the penalty for disobeying health
rules is high enough, even the most stupid people get the
message.

I noticed in China, as I moved out of the hills and across
the fields and into the cities, that as the people became better educated, they were less likely to have epidemics. When
literacy comes in, when even just a few of the leaders are
able to read, they study public health pamphlets and pass
the information on to the people. They begin to ask questions about public health. Why do our children die? What
can we do to prevent these diseases? The mythology is destroyed. They learn that malaria is not due to a damp fog
coming off the river. It's caused by a bite from a mosquito,
and there are things you can do to prevent it.

But it's not just primitive, illiterate people who build mythology around sickness. A Seventh-Day Adventist who drove a truck on the supply convoy along the Burma Road came down with typhus fever. The Adventists in China were a very conservative group; they didn't even eat meat. We got this one into a Red Cross depot and gave him the best nursing possible, but we really wondered if he was going to make it. When he finally began to recover, he confessed to me the real reason why he'd gotten typhus fever. One very cold, rainy night on the Burma Road, when his convoy was about 9,000 feet above sea level, he'd eaten half a tin of bully beef and enjoyed it thoroughly. He was absolutely persuaded in his Seventh-Day-Adventist mind that it was because of this terrible sin that he'd gotten typhus.

I reassured him that he would still have gotten sick even if he'd resisted temptation. Then I told him that what he needed to recuperate was some good, strong liver soup. When he protested, I told him there were two things we could do. We could get vitamin solutions made from liver and put them directly into his veins, or he could get the same thing in the soup. Finally he decided it would be all right as long as it was calf's liver, so I told him I would make the arrangements. But, of course, the Chinese only cooked with pork. So every day, as the other Adventists were having their prayer meeting, the Chinese cook would carry across to him a steaming bowl of soup with great chunks of pig's liver floating in it. The patient recovered, and maybe he learned something, too.

These experiences have convinced me that the secret of fighting any disease, including that new and terrifying one, AIDS, is to educate the population, to give them all the facts and get rid of the mythology.

Sexually transmitted diseases were already a big problem in my doctoring days. Fortunately we could treat VD, al-

though before penicillin that was a long, unpleasant process. It was a common part of our work in the mission hospitals, so common that we automatically did a blood test on
every patient in the hospital. There were so many cases that
we got the manufacturers to put the drug up in big bottles
instead of little, individual ampules for each patient. Then
we just lined the patients up every morning, ten at a time,
and injected them. Many of the other hospitals were quite
intrigued that we could treat VD so cheaply and came to
have a look at our method. It caused quite a sensation.

On the one hand, the program worried some of our more
strait-laced missionaries, who thought that VD was God's
punishment on little Willy for stepping off the duck boards.
We were somehow interfering with God's judgment by curing him. That's still a popular view in certain circles today.

On the other hand, perhaps because people knew there
was a treatment, there wasn't adequate fear of VD. Certainly
there were some horrible cases of gonorrhea in the Chinese
army. When it infected the eyes, it was quick and irrepara-
ble; it could bring total blindness in twenty-four hours. I remember one case in which a soldier went to a brothel where
the women were infected, and, within a week, every soldier
in the platoon was blind. The soldiers didn't know anything
about prevention, and by the time they realized they were
infected, it was too late. It's that sort of frightening example
that's convinced me that we must do everything we can to
educate the public about AIDS.

Somehow we believe that there's something sacred about
keeping people in ignorance. It shows up in our sex education — or rather the lack of it! — and it crops up in the scientific world, too. Scientists are too inclined to say, "I don't
think this is the sort of thing we should tell the public under
the present situation." That's not fair. Scientists owe it to us
to tell us the truth. Meanwhile, the media and our schools

and public health departments are having problems informing people fully about the dangers of AIDS because some people are offended by talk about sex. That's the height of hypocrisy and will only result in misinformation.

Whatever AIDS researchers discover should be released as hot news so that all the information does get out and the public believes it's getting the truth. If we find out that AIDS is more contagious than we thought, let's tell people, even at the risk of having some panic. If we think it's less contagious, let's tell people to relieve their fears.

We must face AIDS in a purely common-sense, scientific manner and get rid of the mythology we're building up about it. One of the myths we need to get rid of is that AIDS is some kind of punishment from God. Maybe AIDS will force us to realize that God doesn't punish people with disease. God is not a snooper, peeking through the bedroom window and hiding behind trees, spying on romantically inclined couples. God is much bigger than that.

Leprosy was in many ways parallel to AIDS. At one time we isolated the leper, and we enforced that isolation by building up a mythology about how contagious leprosy was: it could spread so quickly; even if you touched a leper five years ago, you could still develop it. We made leprosy into a great terror.

The Japanese had a tremendous fear of leprosy, and they still do. One time in Taiwan I was taking a couple of leprosy patients back to their home at the south end of the island where I was going to spend some time showing their local doctor how to treat them. The train left about 8 P.M., so we would spend the night on the train. We arrived early and each took a seat by the window. As the train began to fill up, two smartly dressed Japanese travelling salesmen sat down beside me and one of the lepers. They were very chatty and asked me in English who I was, what I was doing in Tai-

wan, who the fellows with me were. I explained that I was a
doctor and these were patients of mine. "They don't look
sick," the fellow beside me said. "No, they're not very sick," I
said evasively. He kept after me, and finally I said, "Well,
they each have a little bit of leprosy." Both men jumped out
of their seats and shouted. "Leprosy!" and ran out of the car.
The two patients looked around and said, "That's better.
Now we can stretch out on the seat and sleep."

Fortunately the conductor did not hear the shouts or he
might have thrown them off the train, although the Chinese
were not as fearful of leprosy. Sometimes the consequences
of discovery could be quite severe for the leper. When I was
in India, I had 300 or more leprosy patients. Most of them
came to the crowded day clinic, but there were two who visited late at night after I'd finished my evening rounds. One
was high up in the police department, and the other was an
important local official. Their disease had to be kept a secret. I treated them for ten years, and we got away with it. It
was quite exciting, but if either of them had been discovered, he would have been kicked out of the civil service with
no severance pay or pension.

Then leprosy was brought into the open. We told everyone that there was a treatment, that it wasn't that contagious, that there was no need to keep lepers in a colony. And
today, with proper treatment, leprosy is nothing. I always
advised my patients to say that they had a chronic skin disease but that it was under control.

So much of what the leper suffered was because of the
fear other people had of him or her. We may have to go
through that phase with AIDS, of getting all hyped up about
some kid going to school who has antibodies. We get surprisingly panicky when it's *our* health that's at risk. And we
get a curious satisfaction out of that kind of fear. We can an-
chor it all on one person, the scapegoat. We want to have

something or someone we can focus our hatred and fear on, and in some places the AIDS victim is fulfilling that role.

However, let's not forget that sometimes it is necessary to take desperate measures until we have prevention or a cure for a disease. It took centuries to find out how to control leprosy. Probably the stringency with which the leper was treated in Europe helped prevent it from spreading further. The AIDS victim may argue, "I'm living in a free country and I have my rights constitutionally." But on the other hand, sometimes you may have to limit those rights to fight an epidemic. To me, the great crime is not that we interfere with someone's personal liberty. If isolation, for example, will stop the spread of a disease that will interfere with the personal liberty of several hundred people, then it's worth considering.

But will isolation or any other measures that are being proposed be effective? And how widely do they need to be imposed? There is a great danger of overreacting and driving the disease underground. When we used to have isolation for German measles, the mothers would all decide, "If my baby gets measles, I just won't let anybody know about it. The child will be better in two weeks." We don't want that to happen with AIDS. It's hard to know how far we should go. We just have to keep getting as much information as we can and use our common sense.

The person most affected by AIDS is, of course, the male homosexual. Today the homosexual is becoming more willing to identify himself and overcome the social stigma that's existed in the past. That's a very healthy attitude, and it's ironic that this awful threat should have come along at the same time. AIDS will have a profound effect on the homosexual, and in many cases he'll have to rethink his whole lifestyle.

One day a few months ago I was visiting a high school,

and the principal there had just learned that morning that
his nineteen-year-old son was gay. The boy told him quite
sensibly, "Dad, I've done all the reading and I have discovered that I am homosexual. I'm attracted to other men and
I'm not attracted to women. It's just like being left-handed. I
was born with it. You can try to make a left-handed person
right-handed, but he'll end up stuttering or with some other
problem. So I've decided to live my life as a homosexual
with other homosexuals."

I sympathized with that boy and I admired him for his
frankness. One of the great difficulties for the homosexual
has been the psychological problems caused by the fact that
he has to keep his sexual orientation a secret from society.
The problem wasn't his homosexuality. It was society's reac-
tion to his homosexuality. But society is finally getting over
that. We're coming to recognize that it's not a disease, and
as homosexuals are becoming more accepted, I think they
are behaving in a more acceptable manner. The attitude
used to be, "Well, I'm rejected by society anyway, so I might
as well do what I like. I'll never be accepted." Also, since homosexuality is not penalized socially, more of it will surface.
When you read history, you realize that there's been a tremendous amount of homosexuality through the ages, and it
hasn't devastated society.

But now AIDS is going to make it a very difficult thing to
be a practising homosexual. I don't care what precautions
you take, we do not know enough about it to protect ourselves adequately — we may not know enough for several
years yet. Homosexuals will have to consider that and ask
themselves whether it's better to remain celibate and release
their tensions by masturbation. I suspect this is what's happening in China, where the government wants men to wait
before getting married; masturbation is being tolerated and
even recommended there in a way it never was before.

Heterosexuals are at risk, too, and this may force us to finally face up to the problem of prostitution. I don't have the answers, but I sometimes feel that the best way to handle prostitution is to have a designated red-light district, with registered houses, fixed prices and health supervision for strict control of venereal disease. Certainly it's safer for *society* when it's done that way.

This sounds like a terrible suggestion from someone who is supposed to have high moral standards, and I suppose that prostitution can often be a very degrading life. Certainly the ordinary prostitute in a Third World country is a very pitiful creature. But it's interesting that in some of the mature societies where they have legalized prostitution with the proper controls, it seems to work quite well, and the women do not end up suffering some terrible fate.

Because of my gynecology practice, I got acquainted with the prostitutes of every country I went to. For many it was a pathetic existence, but a surprising number of them ended up in terrifically happy marriages. The husband certainly got a very experienced partner. Sometimes he didn't know her background; in other cases he was an ex-customer. It was particularly gratifying to be in their homes and see how happy they were. I suppose the story should have ended in great misery for the person who sinned so badly, but that's not what happened, and somehow the sin seems to have been rather enjoyable. So maybe legalized prostitution with proper controls is something we should take a look at. AIDS is going to force us to rethink many of the assumptions in our society, and perhaps that's not such a bad thing either.

As we look for a cure, there will be many times when we go astray. Leprosy was a marvellous example of public health charging enthusiastically up the wrong path. When public health and statistics developed in the early part of this century, one of the leading statisticians made a map of the world and marked down where leprosy was found. He discovered that it appeared in Norway, Finland, Iceland and only on the coast of China and India. So it was perfectly obvious: leprosy was carried by fish, and all the people who were eating fish were subject to leprosy! For about fifteen years researchers delved into the question of how leprosy was transmitted by fish. Finally someone realized that the reason all the spots on the map were on the coast where the fish-eaters were was because the missionaries hadn't yet gone into the interior and diagnosed leprosy. When they did get to the interior, they found there was just as much leprosy among the meat-eaters. And it was highest of all among the vegetarians.

Leprosy is no longer an expanding disease, and it's no longer looked on with the horror it was 100 years ago. We have abolished smallpox. As soon as people get a decent municipal water supply, they no longer have typhoid. Cholera is probably the cheapest disease in the world to prevent, so there's no reason to ever have a cholera epidemic again. Drugs and insecticides aren't always the perfect solution, but they have enabled us to control malaria, plague, typhus and many other diseases.

These diseases have had their answer, and so will AIDS. Even though we're faced with a desperate situation, I'm tremendously optimistic about AIDS. It's a frightening disease with at least fifty percent mortality — maybe one hundred percent! But I'm convinced that if we put in enough money and get enough brains working on it, we'll find prevention and the cure for AIDS, too.

5

Controlled Compassion

It seems as if every day you read an inspiring story about some heroic and expensive medical miracle. These stories don't impress me. What does impress me is practical, cost-effective medicine. I saw it in the mission field, it's happening in China today, and I believe it has to come back into fashion here.

In the old days in China, when there was a disaster, such as an air raid, the first thing we medical people would have to do was decide on whom we were going to operate. We'd do a quick run down and write off the person who was very badly mangled. We'd give him a huge dose of morphine to relieve his pain, but we didn't spend our effort trying to save him when for the same amount of effort we could probably save the lives of three or four less badly injured people. Otherwise, out of our pity and compassion we would end up spending three hours on a person who had only a twenty-five percent chance of surviving, while other people whom we could have saved died of infection. This approach, known as "triage," is still standard practice during a disaster anywhere in the world.

Judging by what I've seen and heard, what the Chinese are doing today is applying this principle to their whole population. Under the Chinese system, everyone gets the same medical care. And if the medical establishment cannot afford to offer that same level of treatment to everyone, then they don't do it. However, they also practise a version of triage: they only give medical care where it will be of the most benefit to society, as I discovered when I went to visit a "relative" there.

I was the only boy in my family, but I did have an "adopted" Chinese brother, George Washington Wang. I played with him as a child, and while I was in school in Toronto, he lived with my parents back in China. When I returned to China, I had to study Chinese at a school in Beijing because the language I had learned in the streets of China wasn't suitable for a missionary. George was also studying in Beijing, so we renewed our friendship and became "sworn brothers."

After I left China in 1948, I lost track of George; I assumed he was dead. Then, through some friends in Beijing, I learned that at ninety-two he was still alive and wanted to see me before he died. In December 1985 I returned to China to visit him.

It was a wonderful visit, but I was surprised to find that he was quite crippled. He had broken his hip two or three years before and little had been done to fix it. I thought this was a terrible advertisement for Chinese medicine, that a man of such high standing in the community — and a doctor at that! — hadn't had his hip pinned. But to the Chinese this made perfect sense. Pinning a hip is an expensive process. It takes a lot of the surgeon's time, a lot of X-ray time; it's a major operation and the equipment is expensive. If they are going to do a hip operation, they will do it on the person who needs that operation in order to get back into the workforce.

Similarly, Chinese doctors probably wouldn't do open-heart surgery on a person over fifty-five. *Not* because they're afraid of it, *not* because they would be so rough that a fifty-five-year-old person wouldn't survive. But a person that age has fewer years of life ahead of him so he is of less potential use to society than a young, otherwise vigorous person; therefore, to operate on an older person wouldn't be a wise use of their limited medical resources.

At first glance that may seem like a cruel system, but I think it shows a remarkable intelligence — what I call "controlled compassion." The Chinese are not lacking in compassion, but their resources are limited. Therefore, they design their medical budget to give a square deal to everybody and to use their resources where they are most needed and where they will do the most good for society.

I think Western medicine could learn something from that policy because we do *not* always use our resources for the maximum benefit of the greatest number of people. If we do a transplant for a child who has a defective liver, it costs money. We don't quibble about it. How can you put a price on a child's life? But if the child is very young, there's only a fifty percent chance that he or she will survive and grow up to be a normal adult. Meanwhile fifteen million kids, most of them with perfectly good livers — in fact, they're very tough to have survived at all — die every year of starvation. The $100,000 or more that it costs to do the liver transplant would feed a lot of those children, and a quarter of that amount of effort would stamp out an epidemic in the Third World and save the lives of 100,000 children. But those are kids of another shade, and they're way on the other side of the world, and they don't bother us. They die quietly. So, on an international scale, we're not practising controlled compassion.

Another way in which we're misusing our medical budget is spending so much on *curing* health problems but so little on keeping them from happening in the first place. Canadians have some very unhealthy habits. We tend to misuse alcohol and other drugs. We're not in nearly as good shape as we should be. Fortunately, we've finally begun to recognize the importance of exercise, but our general level of fitness is still poor. Can you imagine seeing 1,000 people doing calisthenics before they go to work in the main square of any Canadian city, as they do in China? Most of the Indian businessmen I knew in Ratlam had already spent several hours doing yoga exercises and meditation by the time they got to the office. Think of the difference that makes compared with the person who crawls out of bed after being out late at a party the night before. He drinks some coffee, has no real breakfast, then joins the parade of motorcars, bumper-to-bumper. How do you expect that person to be a leader in his company?

But whose job is it to look after the *preventive* health of the individual? The family doctor? The government? The company he works for? In our society nobody wants someone else interfering with his lifestyle. If you tell him he should stop smoking or join Alcoholics Anonymous, he'll tell you it's none of your business, but when his lungs or his liver go and he can't work anymore, you'll foot the bill.

There is another thing we can learn from the Chinese medical system: the tremendous respect they have for the dignity of the patient. At one Chinese hospital I saw a man come in with his arm all bandaged up and a dead chicken wrapped around it. First, the staff asked him whether he wanted indigenous medicine — herbal medicine, acupuncture and psychotherapy — or Western medicine. It was for *him* to decide. The man asked for indigenous medicine. When the indigenous-medicine doctor unwrapped the arm, it was perfectly obvious that it was broken, so the doctor explained that this was a fracture and that it was better treated with Euro-American methods. "I will take you over and introduce you to the Western-medicine doctor," he explained to the man. What that doctor was really saying was, "You are my patient, and I will see that you get the best possible treatment."

From that incident I learned two things. First of all, that the patient can make choices about his treatment. Secondly, having been chosen, the doctor has an obligation to that patient. It's not like our medical supermarket, where we are told, "You've got the wrong counter, you dummy. Go to the other counter." Here, the patient is often so intimidated by the doctor that even to ask a second opinion is almost an insult. "If you don't want my opinion, why did you come to me?" says the doctor. From the patient's point of view I think it would be so much nicer to feel, "The doctor is really looking after *me*. He's interested in *me*, not just my disease." Nor do practitioners in different disciplines refer patients to each other that way. I'm quite sure there's many a doctor who has a dear old soul with chronic pain in the lower back who would probably get more relief from going to a chiropractor. But how many doctors here would tell a patient to go to a chiropractor?

When I was in private practice in Canada, back in 1949-50, I ended up being an amateur radiologist as well as a surgeon. That was because the radiologist who came to look at our X-rays refused to analyse the ones that had been done for a chiropractor, so the X-ray technician asked me to look at them instead.

Too often Western doctors are chiefly concerned with protecting their status. It's *my* specialty, the dignity of *my* profession that I'm most interested in, not the patient. We all *say* we put the patient first, but in our basic psychology, I think we doctors have often forgotten that .

Where did this habit of glorifying the doctor come from? We've had such an explosion of medical knowledge in the past eighty years that we've come to think of the doctor as the person with all the answers, who can solve any problem. He can give a few shots of insulin to a doomed child, and the kid will recover. He can put a pacemaker into a fellow who is having serious heart problems, and suddenly the man is good for another ten years. Naturally, people think highly of the doctor, and the doctor, being human, begins to think pretty well of himself.

I certainly felt the temptation to glorify myself. I was in places where the general level of education was very low, and I'm sure that unconsciously I enjoyed the adulation I got from my patients. I was introducing modern medicine and hygiene to people who couldn't read or write, and I know I sometimes tended to talk like God. Often I was able to do things that looked like miracles. For example, one day a woman with a ruptured ectopic pregnancy came in. She'd had one sharp blow of pain and then went into complete collapse, and it was obvious she was going to die if she wasn't treated immediately. I gave her a transfusion and tied off the bleeding part in such a way that she could still have children. In a week she went home, completely over it. I was the one who had pulled her back from the edge of the cliff, and I certainly did get a thrill out of something like that.

There were other occasions when my medical behavior was somewhat less than godlike. As a young doctor in China, I had a temporary assignment looking after the employees at a British coal mine. One of my patients there was a Scottish engineer who suffered from a duodenal ulcer. One day a messenger arrived, reporting that Mr. Moffat was suffering from severe stomach pains. I knew he had some bismuth tablets, so I sent a message back that he should take some of this "soda" and that I would come as soon as I could. By noon the messenger was back again, saying that "master was in a bad way." I grabbed my black bag and pedalled off to the engineer's bungalow, expecting he had suffered a perforated ulcer. It was a very hot day. As I came out of the glare of the sun into a dark and stifling room, I found a gasping, unconscious body lying across the bed. I shook him awake. "Doc," he gasped, "I can't take any more soda. I've had five brandy and sodas and three whiskey and sodas. Can't I try something else instead?"

Still, usually I was the great lifesaver, and I could be quite disappointed when somebody reminded me that I was merely human. I would feel a great exhilaration at the success of an operation, and it took a nurse to remind me that that success was the result of teamwork — that without that support I wouldn't have been able to accomplish anything at all. They'd keep me humble.

It was also a great temptation to the missionary to look down on his local colleagues. I was fortunate because right from the beginning it was clear that I was not superior to my Chinese colleagues. When I first arrived in China, my superior was Chinese. Even though he had a lower-class Chinese degree, he had seniority. It was true that I had been sent there to try to improve the level of the surgery, but in return he agreed to teach me how to deal effectively with the Chinese people.

After a while I began to notice that something was bothering Dr. Chang. Eventually I discovered that he was disturbed because I was living in the large mission house while he had a very small house in the Chinese quarters. In a time of growing Chinese nationalism, this was very bad for his "face," his standing in the community. I offered to change houses with him, and he agreed.

I was very happy in my Chinese quarters; they required

very little upkeep or bother. But in the big mission house, Dr. Chang had to hire servants and pay huge bills for heat and water. After just one year, Dr. Chang and his family fled back to the Chinese quarters. "Face" was not that important. However, that incident did teach me not to think of myself as the "big chief."

Looking back on it, I'm very grateful to all my colleagues in medical mission work. They taught me to value teamwork and not to think so much of my own importance. When people said, after a successful operation, "Oh, we're so grateful to you," I learned to say, "Well, it was those fellows in the lab who were able to do the blood typing quickly and give us a proper answer. They were just as important as anything I did with the knife."

Recently, I saw an incident in China that demonstrated the respect that ought to be shown to *all* medical staff, even the most humble. My tour group was visiting a large hospital in north China, a 350-bed hospital, and the chief surgeon was showing us through personally. Since we wanted to see the hospital in action, we didn't let the staff know ahead of time that we were coming. They didn't have time to "whitewash the geese," as we used to say during the war.

When we came to the operating suite, we could read the large sign outside the operating area that said, "Do not proceed beyond this point until you have changed your clothes and shoes." As I looked through the door, I could see a scrub lady with a long-handled mop cleaning up a spill. The chief surgeon excused himself and went in to speak to her. I thought he was going to ask the lady if there was enough clothing and shoes for the eighteen of us to change. But that was not his question. He said to her, "I have eighteen people here from a foreign country and they want to see our operating room. I'm very sorry, but in order to get them to the change room we have to walk over your cleanly mopped floor, and you'll have to mop it again." The lady looked at him, and then she came to attention with her mop, like a soldier on parade, and said, "Doctor, people from foreign countries are always welcome in our hospital, aren't they?" And we all bowed and walked through.

It seemed such a marvellous thing that even the most humble person on the staff could talk to the chief surgeon and call it *our* hospital. The surgeon recognized that if that scrub lady had not been doing a good job in the operating room, it would have been a dirty operation room, and that could have led to serious problems.

How different that is from the way the chief surgeon enters a hospital in Canada. You'll see him coming down the corridor, glowing with rage. He's looking for anything that's wrong. The junior staff all run into the washrooms to get out of his way. Everybody rushes around, saying, "*God* is coming down the corridor", and "*God* had a bad night last night."

Yet one of the most impressive doctors I ever knew was a very humble man, a scientist who made a huge contribution, yet today is virtually forgotten. I met Dr. Robert Pollitzer in 1939 when I returned from furlough in Canada to work with the International Red Cross. He had been with the famous Manchurian Plague Prevention Service. In fact, he'd caught plague himself and recovered from it. I shared a room with him for almost two years. I also kept an eye on him, because he was a very careless eater and we had to make sure that he ate properly. But when it came to his work, he was a very practical man. Whenever we found an epidemic was about to begin, he laid down the law and snuffed it out right at the start.

He continued to work with UNRRA in China after the war, then went on to work for WHO (World Health Organization) in Geneva and a variety of other prestigious organizations, continuing to do research in plague and cholera.

Better-known doctors who have done heroic and glamorous work certainly saved lives, and they have a right to our honor and recognition. But the rare and obscure Dr. Pollitzer saved the lives of millions.

I find that the successful heart-transplant surgeons in Canada also show great humility about their achievements and are tremendously aware of the importance of teamwork. Recently the Muslim community wanted to honor a surgeon at Toronto Western for his work in transplants. The doctor pointed out that they would have to have at least eight other people at the head table. "You must remember that we're a team," he explained. "And we also represent many people who have been working on transplants for years and whose research we were able to use."

Technology, I think, is bringing us back to that understanding of teamwork in medicine. For example, the orthopedic surgeon doing an operation relies not just on his own skills, but on the technician who uses his equipment to diagnose the problem, the researcher who discovers new materials that can be used for sutures and artificial ligaments, and the physiotherapist who will bring the patient to fullest possible use of his limbs.

My son-in-law had heart surgery recently, and it was interesting to see the tremendous mutual support among all the medical staff. The heart surgeon realizes that sooner or later the fate of his patient is going to depend on a nurse who's watching twelve little screens. If there's any abnormality, she's the one who has to jump on it right away. So as our system becomes more complicated, it's essential that everyone feel part of the team, because the system is only as strong as its weakest link.

However, it's not only the nurses and technicians who need to be recognized, to feel that what they are doing is essential. Doctors need respect, too. I no longer have much contact with the medical establishment in Canada. I often speak to doctors and medical students as a group, but not as individuals. Nevertheless, I have a sense that they're discontented, that something is missing, and I think that something is the feeling of being needed.

I know from my own experience what a terrific difference that sense of being essential makes. It was the *need* of a place that made me want to go there, and it was the satisfaction of meeting that need that repaid me, because I certainly didn't get repaid financially. When I returned to Canada I found the situation was different. It wasn't long till I got very frustrated. As a doctor I was not meeting any particular need. I was not the sole resource for any patient. If I wasn't there the patient could just ring the doorbell on the other side of the hall and see the doctor there. If the patient didn't like the service I was giving him, if I was too busy one time and told him to call somebody else, I might lose that patient for good.

Consequently, the individual doctor today often doesn't get satisfaction out of his work. He's not essential. There are "umpteen" life preservers — the whole deck's crowded with them. The wealthy communities of southern Canada have a surplus of doctors, and that affects the respect that the patient has for a doctor, and therefore the way the doctor feels about himself or herself.

Perhaps the respect we naturally have for doctors has been spoiled by a few who have been too conscious of the financial rewards, but I don't think that's because doctors are more greedy than the rest of us. The high income, I believe, is a compensation. If the doctor isn't getting the respect, the gratitude that he anticipated when he entered the profession, sometimes he must feel that making a lot of money will more or less repay him for the work he does. He's not getting repayment in any other currency.

In other parts of the world, most doctors still enjoy a tremendous image, but that image is not necessarily reflected in their salaries. The doctor in Japan is very respected, but he works long hours for relatively small return financially. In China, the newly graduated doctor starts out with the same image as a motor mechanic, and the most outstanding doctors are paid probably five dollars a month more than the bus driver. But they have the definite respect and affection of the public.

Doctors all over the Third World seem to be highly motivated by things other than money — maybe by this desire for respect, maybe out of a humanitarian urge, maybe from a need to advance their families' standing. One group that I remember as being particularly highly motivated were the students at the hospital in Gaza. By 1952 we had trained a whole class of refugee kids in laboratory and X-ray technology. With this background they could go almost anywhere in the Arab world and find jobs. And they were willing to go because then they could become citizens of their adopted countries rather than being stuck as refugees on that tiny strip of land.

To sell these technicians, I travelled along the coast of North Africa, over the old World War II battlefields, to Libya. I knew that Libya, which was then ruled by King Idris, had a tremendous need for technical people. The minister of health said he would take all we had, but please, please, could I find him an Arab doctor, preferably a surgeon, to work in the national health service.

At that time we had on our staff a fine young surgical resident, Octav Habash, who had graduated from the French Medical College in Beirut. He agreed enthusiastically that he would go to Libya. We made up a contract, sent it off, and then waited for the bureaucracy to process his papers. In the meantime, we operated together three days a week. If we were doing an operation on a woman, I told him to think of the patient as the Queen of Libya. I would say, "When you put a clamp on an artery, do it carefully, and when you tie the artery off, do it very securely. Say to yourself, 'We are just making sure, Your Highness.' " On a male patient we would say, "Have patience, Your Majesty. We are just being extra careful."

The contract came through, and Habash left for Libya, where he soon became chief surgeon in the National Health service. We corresponded for a while, but both of us were very busy and we soon lost touch.

About three years later I was back in Toronto for my father's 100th birthday party. There were many cards and telegrams from all around the world where Dad's former medical students were now working. Among them was one very heavy envelope with a colorful embossed crest, covered with exotic stamps. The card inside read, "On the occasion of Dr. William McClure's 100th birthday, King Idris and the Royal Family wish to join in extending hearty congratulations. Sent by Dr. Octav Habash, Physician-in-Ordinary to the Royal Family." Down in the corner was a little handwritten note: "P.S. I am very careful."

I doubt if we'll be able to arrange that level of motivation for all our young doctors, but I wonder if motivation isn't something we should place more emphasis on, especially with the increasing technology in medical education. We always think of the old doctor who knew his patients so well, but I'm not sure we're making those kind of doctors anymore. We are training a great number of high-grade medical technicians, there's no doubt about that. But do they know as much about their patients as they do about the latest lab tests? Are they motivated by a spirit of service or just by a desire to do well and make money?

Often when we decide who's going to get into medical college, we don't look at the students' motivation. The marks are put in the computer, the buttons are pushed, and the top 100 come out; they go into the class and that's it. But I know from my own experience that it isn't always obvious who will be a good doctor.

Antonio Boba was about the least promising student I ever dealt with. He came from an Italian ex-patriate family in Cairo and had managed to graduate from some second-rate medical schools in Europe. He came to work at the hospital in Gaza, green as grass, but terribly interested in the mechanical aspects of medicine. He set up an automatic pentothal drip system for anesthesia and built a machine for distilling our water. As a doctor and surgeon, however, I thought he was very lightweight. Still, I filled out a strong recommendation that he be accepted for an internship at a hospital in Connecticut. Within three years he was working as an anesthetist in Syracuse, New York. He became head of the department and wrote a book, *Death in the Operating Room*, about the problems of anesthetics. Yet, if we hadn't given him a chance, and if he hadn't had the drive to make the best of that chance, he probably would never have become a successful doctor.

In the past, medical colleges seemed to pay more attention to the character of the student. One outstanding medical educationalist in Canada was Wendell Macleod. When he was dean of the medical college in Saskatoon, he would have an intensive interview with every applicant. He was trying to judge if this was the kind of student who should be in a medical college. Even if the student didn't have top marks, if MacLeod thought that he would make a good doctor, he would bend the rules to get the kid into the school. Compassion and common sense were more important than having an average that was one-tenth of a percent higher than everybody else's.

I think that in the old days, when classes were smaller and the staff had a very definite image of what a doctor ought to be, this sort of evaluation was more common. There were also certain courses where the professor wielded the axe.

In my day at the University of Toronto, chemistry was the course in which they weeded out the boys they didn't think had the right stuff. The professor of chemistry was a very astute man who could figure out the character of the student by the kind of work he did in the chemical lab. He would feel quite free to fail someone if he didn't feel the student would make a good doctor. A boy I knew failed three times in first-year medicine. His father was a missionary and squandered money trying to get the kid through first year, but it was obvious the staff had decided that although the boy's marks were good enough, he would not have been a capable doctor.

I don't think that kind of weeding out is possible now. Even the examinations are all multiple-choice questions. Any kid from high school could correct the paper. You'd be in a lot of trouble if you failed the student who seemed to be very bright technically but who had some moral flaw. I don't think today's staff would see that as a reason for failing someone. Yet a highly motivated doctor can make such a difference, not just to his patients, but to a whole society. We all know about the work of Dr. Norman Bethune, but China has an even more striking example of a dedicated and revolutionary doctor.

During the war years in China we often heard about a strange "Dr. Ma." Some said he was a mythical person. Others thought he was a mixture of several different personalities. Surely all those stories couldn't be true of one person. Others suggested he was a fast-talking quack doctor who had managed to endear himself to the revolutionary leadership. Then the "bamboo curtain" came down, and we heard no more. It was not until the late 1970s that I discovered Dr. Ma was a real person. I got into correspondence with him, and then in 1981 met him on a trip to Beijing. This was his story.

In 1939 Ma Hai-Teh was a young doctor with a dream of helping suffering humanity. At that time, the humanity that was suffering the most were the Communists. They were surrounded by Chiang Kai-Shek's army, and no drugs could get through to them. Their medical problems were terrible; even the wounded could not be looked after. So Ma Hai-Teh joined the army. There he met Mao Tse-tung, Chou En-Lai and the other Communist leaders. Although he wasn't a Communist to start with, Dr. Ma found he could support their principles, and when the army retreated to North China, he went with them.

Even during the worst times, the Communist leaders were making plans for what they would do after their victory, and much of the medical content of those plans came from Dr. Ma. Even though he had had no special training in public health, he saw things from that angle, just as the revolutionaries did. If something was wrong, they didn't want to just solve the individual cases; they wanted to change the system.

Dr. Ma's plans included immunization programs, inexpensive improvements in sanitation and control of venereal disease through the army. Soldiers were the most common victims of VD, and since they would pass on what they learned to their friends and family, educating the soldiers about VD meant educating the whole country. Ma virtually wiped out prostitution in Shanghai, moving the women into clothing factories, where they could make far more money sewing army uniforms than they ever could on the streets. He cleared up kala-azar, a disease that killed thousands of children, with just a few doctors and nurses, by training local people to recognize and treat it.

Dr. Ma never tried to ignore or hush up China's health problems. He had doctors who were very knowledgeable in public health and who had free rein to do their work — he was not a one-man show at all. He won the respect of the Chinese leaders, so that after 1949, whatever he ordered was law.

But perhaps the strangest thing I discovered about the mysterious Dr. Ma was that he wasn't Chinese at all. Ma Hai-Teh was the Chinese translation for George Hatem, an American doctor whose compassion had transformed not only his own life, but an entire country.

6

God Speaks to Everyone

I'm not subject to auditory hallucinations like little Samuel in the Bible, who heard God calling him in the middle of the night, but I do believe that God speaks to people.

One of the most dramatic examples of this that I've come across was when I was visiting at the University of Western Australia in 1974. While I was there, I met a professor of anatomy who had just returned from Ethiopia. Professors of anatomy are usually the least enthusiastic people you could imagine, but Professor Albrook was full of excitement about his trip. He explained that he and his wife had been watching TV one night about six months ago when a program came on, a real tearjerker about the troubles in Ethiopia — war, famine, disease. They were quite stirred by it. When the program was over, the professor got up, turned off the TV, and just stood there. "Well, what are you going to do?" his wife said. "You used to be a surgeon. And they need surgeons."

It was Friday night. The professor and his wife started phoning right then and there. He got a six-month leave of absence and left Monday afternoon on a plane supplied by the Australian air force, loaded with six resident doctors from the university hospital and four or five tons of medical supplies. For six months he led a relief surgical unit right in the war zone of Ethiopia. Meanwhile, Mrs. Albrook kept things going back home, raising money, finding supplies, getting other medical people involved. When the professor's time was up, somebody else volunteered to take his place. In the end, the program went on for two years.

To me, their experience was a tremendous example of how God calls people today, not in a hocus-pocus sort of way, but through a TV program, a newspaper article, a conversation with a friend.

Most people think of a call as a once-in-a-lifetime thing — something very grand and adventurous that makes a good Sunday-school story. Sometimes a call *is* like that, but I believe that calls are coming all the time. We are always having to make choices about what we're going to do next with our lives. You may suddenly get the urge to abandon the family farm to start a subsistence agriculture program in Bangladesh. You might be inspired to volunteer at your local hospital or learn to be a better parent to your kids. Whatever it is, it's a call, and you'll get a thrill out of responding to it.

I've made a lot of these choices in my life, and though sometimes they completely destroyed my well-laid plans, I've never regretted my decision.

One such call happened when I was studying medicine in Toronto. I had always wanted to be a medical missionary like my father, but I knew that he was forever short of books and equipment and supplies, so I had the angles all worked out. I was going to take a job in the British Colonial service. This was a very secure job, which paid extra for the great sacrifice of living abroad. My plan was to suffer in the South Seas for about ten years or so, save up a little nest egg, then, when I was able to buy all the books and special equipment I needed, go back to mission work.

One day my shrewd plans blew up. Dr. Pidgeon, the minister at Bloor Street Presbyterian, called me. Dr. Menzies in Hwaiking had been killed by bandits. Would I go out and replace him? It was a marvellous idea! I was disappointed that World War I had ended before I was old enough to enlist, and I thought it would be so glamorous to be back in China, being shot at. It didn't take me ten minutes to decide. In fact, I think it alarmed Dr. Pidgeon that I was so eager.

I have never had any question that that was a call from God and that I *had* to respond to it. There were many more to come. If you respond to one call in your life, you become more sensitive to calls. You'll respond to another, and then another. Something always opens up. But if you don't respond, the next time the call isn't quite so loud, and eventually the calls don't come anymore. Your calling apparatus is out of order.

That's very sad because it's such a marvellous thing to have a sense of purpose and that shared excitement with other people who may be responding to the same challenge. But what a soggy sort of existence it is to lack that feeling that you're doing what you were meant to do. You're grinding out your daily work, but there's no glamor in it. It's just plain hard slogging compared to people who are doing something because they feel it's especially right for them.

Of course, if it's a true call, it will be something you're suited for. You can't just go out on an adventure without any preparation, hoping you'll learn as you go along. Often I've found that when something needs doing, I've already had the training or experience to do it.

A good example was the air-ground rescue program my Red Cross unit set up during World War II. Allied air crews that went down in the "Hump," the mountain area between

China and Burma, never returned. They were lost or injured or possibly killed by the local tribal people, who viewed any outsider as an enemy. The Allied air forces didn't seem to be interested in solving the problem. They thought that the best way to deal with the tribal people was to shoot them. If anything was going to be done, it looked like we'd have to do it ourselves.

I'd had both pilot training and parachuting with the Norwegian air force and I knew the area well. So I set out to get a liaison in every tribal village and persuade the people to look after the flyers, to either take them out to the Burma Road, where we could pick them up, or notify us so that we could parachute in and look after them ourselves. In return, we took about one medical case from each of the villages, treated them in the hospital and sent them back again. The program ran for two years, and we recovered about twenty flyers.

Looking back, I realize that doing that program was definitely a call, and one that I had anticipated by taking flying and parachuting lessons. I had an idea that some program like this might be needed. If not, the training was good fun and I might have used it some other time.

All of us have special talents or skills or experience that can be useful. Many people will think this sounds simplistic — "socialism lesson number one" — but I believe those abilities also bring obligations. If you've got a good education, it's usually acquired at the expense of the public, so you owe them something in return. If you're in a position of power, that power isn't just for you to enjoy. It's for you to use responsibly. And so on. However, I don't believe that this responsibility should be a burden because, in my experience, no matter what you're called to do in life, you get the greatest kick out of being able to serve others. And the greater the other person's need, and the less the reward you get for it, the greater the pleasure you get.

I've forgotten all about the big operations I did in my career. Sometimes I even wonder if I really did them. What I remember are the people, and some of the people I most enjoyed treating were lepers. Nobody else wanted to treat them. There was no line-up of doctors waiting to get their hands on the lepers. Moreover, people suffering from leprosy were very poor. They couldn't express their thanks with even the simplest gift.

I began doing leprosy work in Taiwan in 1927. Amy and I had just been married and we had gone over to Taiwan to escape the civil war in China. Dr. Taylor, who was the chief of the hospital there, taught me how to diagnose and treat the disease. Every Saturday we had 660 lepers. I took the kids under fifteen, and he took the rest. We worked from eight o'clock in the morning till four or five in the evening. It was tremendously thrilling. There was no sure cure in those days. We just injected the lepers with chalmoogra oil. Out of the 330 kids I had, we thought it was wonderful if at the end of the year five of them were in remission. It should have been frustrating work but, because I felt so needed, I got a lot of satisfaction out of it.

Later, in India, I had a chance to work with lepers again, but this time we had better treatments. I particularly liked rebuilding the sunken noses that were the mark of the leper. I came to realize that I was not remaking a nose at all — I was remaking a person! The classic case was a little Muslim lady. She had claw hands and twisted feet and a very conspicuous leprosy nose. Treating her reminded me of the mechanic who once told me that to fix my car I should jack up the horn and drive a new body and engine underneath.

I explained to her what needed to be done and asked her what we should do first. I thought she would say, "Do my right hand." But instead she said, "Do my nose. On my lousy feet I can only walk ten miles a day and I live thirty miles away and I can't take the bus. I can hide my hands and I can hide my feet, but my nose gives me away. As soon as I get on the bus, everybody shouts, 'Leper!' and the conductor throws me off and I have to walk. If you could fix my nose, then I could take the bus." She was one of our first cases, and the results were beautiful. It was a very dramatic example of how one could change someone's whole life by an operation. She was no longer a leper. She was a person.

A case like that is gratifying because one feels so *useful*. Now, not everyone is called to do things that other people will think are exciting. But you can still get satisfaction out of life if you feel that you are serving other people. Secretaries and bank tellers must often get depressed because people tell them their jobs aren't important enough, that they should go into law or some other glamorous job. But secretaries and bank tellers and bus drivers and the guy who puts on the third coat of enamel over at the Ford plant are all useful members of society. We'd have a hard time getting along without them. Still, if you're not getting a deep satisfaction out of what you're doing in life, if you don't feel like an important member of the team, maybe you should make some changes. Maybe you should be listening for a call to do something more.

I think life is organized so that there is always a door open somewhere. It may not be the nicest door. It may look risky or unpleasant. But if it needs to be done and if you know somehow that it's right for you, you'd better take it anyway. Because if you can face those risks or problems and overcome them, you begin to get a tremendous confidence in yourself and in God.

Sometimes I've had doubts about some of the calls I've answered. Sometimes the choices I've made have forced me to change my ideas or my way of doing things. For example, when I went to work with a group of Quakers on the Burma Road, I wasn't sure I'd make a very good pacifist. Up to that time I'd always worked in bandit and guerrilla country, so I'd carried a little pistol in my pocket. It was a nice handy thing to have — it gave me a feeling of assurance. If some bandit came along, I'd at least have a sporting chance. Fortunately, I had only had to use it once, and that wasn't to shoot anyone. It happened during the first air raid I was ever in. A group of people were getting off a ferry on the Yellow River when I spotted a Japanese plane heading for us. I yelled, "Lie flat! Lie flat!" Some of them were a bit slow, so I fired my pistol over their heads. That got a quick response! Just then the plane swooped in and fired at them. If they'd been standing up, they certainly would have been hit.

Many of the missionaries did have guns of some type, but there was always some debate about whether or not we should be carrying them. Of course, when I went to join the Friend's ambulance unit, I knew I would have to get rid of mine (Quakers are pacifists), so I sold it to a captain in the British commandos. It was an automatic, and people were always getting in trouble with those pistols because you couldn't tell whether or not they were loaded. I told the commando, "For heaven's sake, be careful with it." We were staying at a Chinese guest house. After we'd finished our transaction, I went in to have my dinner. A little while later there was a shot. It came right through the bamboo partition and missed the mayor of the town by six inches. Somebody told him it was McClure's gun, and he was absolutely furious. I had to explain very quickly that it wasn't my gun anymore. Maybe it was a lucky thing for me that my new calling had forced me to give up that pistol. As it turned out, I got along fine without it.

As a surgeon, I usually felt fairly well qualified to take on the projects I've been assigned to, but that hasn't stopped me from making mistakes. Sometimes you may also be called to do a job that's grossly beyond your ordinary capacity. There's no one else to do it, so you just do your best. You may not succeed — the patient dies or the project fails — but at least you did your best. So for heaven's sake, don't lie awake at night worrying about it. Go on to the next job. That's psychological equipment you need to have — the ability to keep moving forward.

I learned something about that also when I was working on the Burma Road. One time when we were out flying over the mountains, night came on before we could reach home. So we had to decide whether to come down on the Indian side of the mountains or the Chinese side. I persuaded the pilot to go down on the Indian side, where there were good supplies and for once I could get some ham and eggs for breakfast. But the next morning that plane was sent off on another mission. How was I going to get back to China? I went to the Americans, who said, "You're wearing an RAF uniform. Go on over and get the Brits to help you." I went over to the British. They said, "You're not carrying any orders, so we can't help you."

Finally, because I was desperate, the Americans said, "There's a plane over there that's just about to leave. You can hitch a ride on it." I got all my stuff together and jumped on board. Although I had my parachute with me, which I folded myself and took everywhere, I noticed that none of the four flyers had any parachutes. I figured they had them stowed in back somewhere. There was a big, closed-off area behind us, but no one said anything about it, so I figured it was one of those things everybody kept hush-hush. After a while one of them said, "I see you've brought your parachute." I said, "Yeah, where's yours?" Then he laughed and said, "See that behind you? That's eight tons of aviation fuel. If anything happens to us, we won't need parachutes. " Now I knew why there hadn't been any line-up for my seat on the plane!

A little while later I asked where the facilities were. They told me I had to go down a sort of tunnel under the gas tank and open a door at the other end. I crawled down the tunnel and felt around in the dark, but though I tried and tried, I couldn't get the door open. Finally I inched my way back and complained about it. "You old fool, " the captain said. "You have to close the door behind you and lock it first. It's a safety feature. Once you do that, the door in front will open by itself."

I think that's the way it often is in life. When you can't get a new door open, it's usually because you've left the back door open so you can sneak out that way if you want to escape. But if you close the old door firmly behind you, God will open a new one in front of you.

7

Is There Life After Retirement?

Just as there's a time when you're called to do something, there's also a proper time to stop doing it and move on to another kind of life. If you don't, you're going to cause problems for yourself and others.

My father gave me some good advice about retirement in the form of a story. In the 1920s he was working as the head of the department of internal medicine at a Christian medical college in China. One day his second-in-command came to Dad with a problem. "I've had an offer to go to the University of Hong Kong, " he explained. "After a year or two I'll probably be made dean of medicine." The salary, of course, would be much higher. But, in spite of everything, the younger man said, he would rather remain at the college if he could look forward to taking over Dad's position in the near future.

Dad was sixty-seven, past retirement age; his appointment was renewed year by year; his health was excellent. (He lived to be a hundred, so clearly there was still a lot of tread left on the tire.) He spoke fluent Chinese, so all of his lectures were in the local language, and he had translated

most of the books used by the students. Although his second-in-command was less fluent in Chinese, he was outstanding in tropical diseases, and his departure would have
been a real loss for the school.

"That's no problem at all, " said my father. "I'll retire and
you'll become head of internal medicine just as fast as we
can put it through." And that's what happened. Dad stayed
on as professor emeritus for more than ten years. When my
mother died, he often had his meals with the younger professor and his wife and even stayed in their house for a
while. It was a very happy relationship — almost like a father and son — but it could only have happened because my
father knew how to retire when the time came. I got the message. I made up my mind right then that I would retire as
soon as I hit sixty-six.

Many older people disagree with me. They don't see why
they should retire when they're still healthy and competent.
But my Dad's message was that if you don't retire, you may
be blocking the ladder for someone else. By clinging to your
job, you may be holding someone back, both in their career
and financially. Besides, if you insist that you can't be
forced to retire, how is your company ever going to get rid
of you? The only way would be to fire you for professional
incompetence. That could lead to an endless lawsuit — and
what a way to quit an organization or career to which you
may have given your whole life!

A good example of a man who overstayed his welcome
was the president of Singapore. Dr. Benjamin Sheares was
the leading gynecological surgeon in the Commonwealth
when I studied with him in the late 1950s. Because there was
mandatory retirement in Singapore, he became professor
emeritus when he reached sixty-five. Then, after a couple of
years, the government made him the president of Singapore,
a ceremonial position similar to being Governor General in

Canada. At first he was a terrific president. They'd never had such an energetic man. But ordinarily the president only stays in office for three, at most four, years. When I went back to Singapore again, he had been in office for seven years. His good relationship with the people and the government was wearing very thin, and he was no longer appreciated. How much better it would have been if there had been a legal limit to his term!

Our problem in Canada is that we see retirement as something demeaning, as losing face. We have to leave because we're no good for anything anymore. We need to acquire a more mature attitude to retirement. I've noticed such a contrast when I've visited England or Sweden or other older countries. I've met people who *boast* that they're retired, and I've seen the wonderful work they do as volunteers.

In 1938 I went to Sweden to see the great explorer Sven Hedin, who gave me his maps of Mongolia and Tibet. He had worked his retirement out carefully, putting most of his money into building a six-apartment complex in the suburbs of Stockholm. This provided him with housing and enough money to live on and freed him to travel and give lectures on the sociology and anthropology of Mongolia and Tibet.

On another visit to Sweden I noticed that the policemen, who were all dressed like admirals, had little flags on their shoulders. When I asked one of them what the flags were for, he explained that they indicated what languages each of the officers could speak. I thought I had him stumped. "What if someone from China were hit by a car? Do you have anyone who speaks Chinese?"

The policeman got out a little book, flipped through the pages then said, "I'd phone Professor Andersen."

I said, "Do you think he really speaks Chinese?"

The officer said, "Let's phone him and find out."

Sure enough, when Professor Andersen got on the phone and I started jabbering away to him, he spoke perfect Chinese.

When I went to see him, I found out that he was a retired missionary who had been terribly interested in Chinese literature and art. He was then in his eighties, but he still made use of his expertise as a volunteer. Whenever anyone was being sent out to China, he would give that person language lessons. If anyone from China was coming to visit, Professor Andersen would act as his host. And there were similar volunteers for every language. What a thrill it must have been for those volunteers to feel that they were useful, that they weren't on the shelf, that they were keeping up their contacts!

The key to a happy retirement is feeling that you're still useful. One of the signs of aging is when a person who is still healthy, still financially sound, starts getting grouchy. Five years ago he was active and enthusiastic, but now he doesn't seem to respond to anything. Why? Because he's stopped doing for other people. He's concentrating on himself. It's "my" bowling club, "my" bridge group. It's all "me" being entertained — and not being useful to anyone.

The person who has had to retire and hasn't prepared for it thinks that because he's not going to be carrying great responsibility, he's useless. This is a universal syndrome affecting all senior citizens, and it's a terrifically depressing idea. I've actually had people ask me to bring them a pill to put them out of their misery. "You understand my condition," they say, "and you know that I'm of no use to anybody and nobody loves me." But if they'd be useful to somebody, then somebody would love them.

In more traditional societies, older people had certain obligations. In China, grandmothers work hard, looking after the mending, making new clothes, often teaching the grand-children to do these things. This is particularly true today when often both parents are working. The granddaughter of my adopted brother, George Wang, came to North America to do post-graduate work. While she was here, she met another Chinese student and married him. A year later they had a baby. What were they to do? Both were here on schol-arships, doing advanced technical studies. They had no time to look after a baby and no money to pay someone else to do it. So during the Christmas holidays, when the baby was three months old, the father took the child, along with a load of diapers and bottles, back to Tientsin, to the grand-parents. The grandparents would look after the baby for the next two years until the parents finished their studies. There were no questions asked. That's the natural function of grandparents.

But in Canada, where the extended family is not so strong, where Grandma and Grandpa may live on the other side of the country, we don't feel that responsibility. We need to have something to take its place, a sense of obliga-tion toward society. Senior citizens can then say to them-selves, "I'm living in Burnaby — or Wolfville, or the Parkdale district of Toronto — and this is my community and I have a job to do here, whether it's leading a Brownie pack or serving Meals on Wheels."

In fact, with the retirement age going down and the num-ber of older people increasing and our government deficits going up all the time, I think senior citizens are duty-bound to serve the community, perhaps even doing some of the things that in the past have been done by salaried people, such as, looking after public gardens and buildings. A se-nior citizen who's hard up might get an apartment in return for being a building superintendent. Someone who's been a good basketball player could work as a coach. And the way

our society is going, we'll need many men to serve as Big
Brothers, because there are many big fathers who run away!

For many years there has been a group of retired people
in Peterborough who do household repairs for those who
can't do that kind of thing for themselves — putting up
storm windows, repairing appliances. The people who do it
get a tremendous kick out of it because they feel useful.
Even if a fellow's only fixing a leaky tap, he still feels loved,
because if it weren't for him, the tap wouldn't get fixed.

Some people tend to downgrade volunteer work. Often
when I go into a philanthropic office or a political organization, it seems to be in total disarray. The files are all over the
place and they can't find the letter I wrote them. And what's
their excuse? "Oh, we're dependent on volunteers."

There's no reason why volunteers should be any less competent than anyone else who's doing important work. In
wartime, the "dollar-a-year" man was often the best help
you could get. One of the most efficient leaders I ever had
the pleasure to work for was a volunteer at Oxfam in Britain. He was a retired major in the British army who became
the number two man in the overseas department. His office
ran flawlessly, and once in a blue moon, at his own expense,
he'd fly out to Kenya or some such place to see how a certain project was getting on. He was having a whale of a time,
he was doing excellent work, and he didn't cost the organization a cent.

George Cadbury is another good example of a man who
was every bit as effective as a retired volunteer as he was
when he was an executive in business and at the U.N. At age
fifty-five he became a full-time, unpaid volunteer serving on
the executive and governing bodies of International
Planned Parenthood and also as treasurer of the NDP.
Then when he was seventy he retired from his *volunteer* jobs.
He's still active in family planning and other causes, but he

knew that younger people were waiting to take over and would probably do a more effective job.

When Gordon Bates, the founder of the Health League of Canada, gave up his private medical practice, he continued to put in a full week at the league. It was he who persuaded Canadians that inoculation was not just for well-to-do people who knew a good pediatrician. It was for everyone. And as a retired man he was able to speak out frankly when children died unnecessarily from diseases they could have been inoculated against. I used to see him when I was home on leave from the mission field, and as long as I can remember he was the lifeblood of the Health League.

I did a great deal of volunteer work overseas after my retirement, and nobody ever implied that because I was a volunteer I probably wasn't a good doctor. In fact, I sometimes found it gave me an advantage. The most dramatic example was in Borneo, where I was in charge of the last mission hospital in Malaysia. We were negotiating with Major-General Ishmail, the minister of health, to turn the hospital over to the government. For the most part the negotiations went very well. Even though the government was Muslim, Major-General Ishmail insisted that not a single member of our Christian staff was to leave. "You have a very special spirit here, and we want it to be perpetuated," he told us. However, one time, in working out some of the details, he became rather emphatic and began to pound the table, saying, "This is the way it must be done!" I said, "Now just a minute, General. You are here because you were sent; I am here because I volunteered. I think we can talk about this quietly without any table-thumping."

I was so glad to be able to say that. If I hadn't been a volunteer, I could have been accused of protecting my own job, of clinging to a position that could have gone to a young Malayan. But as it was, no one could question my motives.

And the Major-General and I became great friends — in fact, we still exchange Christmas cards.

As well as getting satisfaction out of serving others, I think that retirement is an opportunity to do some unique work of your own, something perhaps that you've always wanted to do but have never had time for. I know a retired farmer who was always good with his hands but who was too busy doing the chores to take up any kind of hobby. Now he does very delicate work in wooden inlay. He doesn't do it for money but just for the personal satisfaction; and he'll throw out piece after piece until he thinks he's done something good enough to keep. He's worked for other people all his life; now he can get a sense of personal achievement. Another man in his nineties always regretted that he never got to finish high school, so now he's taking classes at university. The critical thing is that these people have not *surrendered* to being old.

Nevertheless, if you're going to be useful in your retirement, and if you're going to enjoy it, you have to start planning it early. I learned this back in 1927, when Amy and I were forced to spend three years in Taiwan because of the violence in China. My chief at the hospital in Taipei had asked me to look after the foreign community. He didn't want to tend to them himself because he didn't like their lifestyle. Many of them were living with Chinese women, and they also tended to be heavy drinkers — *not* the missionary type. But it didn't bother me. Amy and I made some good friends among the younger couples who had just arrived from England. When those kids got together in the evening, what would they talk about? What they were going to do when they retired! Some of them were even younger than we were. In Canada, only old people talked about retirement.

We got to know one couple in particular. They were interested in boats but didn't want to live in the country, so they had decided to retire in a town where they could have a house near the canals and keep a boat. When the war came along, they had to leave Taiwan. Later we went to visit them, and everything had turned out exactly as they had planned. He was the air raid warden, and she was working with the people who had fled from the bombing in London. Even then they were making plans to move to a condominium in the suburbs of London when they got too old to look after their house. We were back to visit them recently, and, sure enough, everything had gone exactly according to schedule. I've never seen such happy people. An important part of that happiness was careful financial planning. They've never been wealthy, but they've always lived within their means and never been a burden to anyone.

Meeting these people had a profound effect on both Amy and me. We said to ourselves, "Well, if they can plan their retirement, we can too." We realized that we would not be able to live a very jolly life on our pension alone. So once we had paid for the kids' education, we hired a broker and gave him complete power to manage our savings while we were abroad. We told him we wanted our money to work as hard as we did. We realized that involved some risky investments, and we were willing to let him take those risks.

We owe a great debt of gratitude to him, because when we finally came to retire in 1966, we were in good shape financially. At that time, we switched everything into more secure investments. I've been surprised at how little worry we have over money, especially when I see what has happened to colleagues who had about the same salary but who haven't planned ahead.

It's a good thing we had that lesson in Taiwan, because, let's face it, the present generation of senior citizens was very ill-prepared to meet retirement. We weren't trained for

it; we didn't have much literature on it. We're getting it now,
but it's very late. It's going to people whose minds are already made up, whose patterns are already set, whose habits
are formed. People should start learning about retirement
and old age very early, perhaps even in public school.

Many friends of ours took retirement classes, but somehow it just didn't sink in. They didn't really make plans or
give it any serious thought. Then suddenly at sixty-five the
axe fell, and they were devastated. One of my friends just
hung around the house for the first two weeks, driving his
wife crazy. "George, for heaven's sake, *do* something!" she
finally said. "Get out-of-doors, get out of my way, get something to do!" And the only thing George could think of to do
was to jump in the car and drive down to the parking lot
and watch the boys come into the office in the morning. To
me, that's an utter failure to adapt to retirement, and it's
tragic.

Even though I prepared myself in some ways, I really always thought old age was something that happened to other
people. It's like in war. When the colonel tells you, "One in
every two of you is going to be wounded," the first thing you
do is look at the fellow next to you and think, "The poor
sod." Now, when I visit seniors' homes and see the shape
some of them are in, I'm surprised, perhaps a little depressed. Some of what has happened to them is unavoida-
ble, but some of it is also preventable — if they had taken
the trouble to keep their bodies and minds in shape.

As a doctor, I was always preaching to my patients and
students that a healthy lifestyle would lead to a healthy old
age. The McKay Hospital where I worked in Taiwan was a
teaching hospital, so I often took medical students on my
rounds. One time a rather elderly man came into the outpatient clinic complaining of a cough. I listened very carefully,
but the cough was not that bad. In fact, the man was in very

good shape, even though he was about seventy, which was old for Taiwan in those days. The students were crowding around, and I thought this was an ideal opportunity to teach them a lesson in good health habits.

I asked him, "Do you smoke?"

"Oh, no," he replied. "I used to smoke a lot, maybe three packs a day. But I quit that about twenty years ago. You can't smoke like that and be in the good shape I'm in today."

The lesson was going well. "Do you drink?" I asked.

"Oh, no. I drank heavily for several years, but when I was about forty I swore off. A man can't drink alcohol and have a good body like I have at seventy."

I asked him if there were any women in his life.

"Oh, no. I had a wife and a couple of concubines. But I gave all that up some years ago. I don't think you can fool around with a lot of women and have a healthy body at seventy."

By this time, all the students were crowding in to hear the message. "To what do you attribute this wonderful health at seventy years of age?" I asked.

And he said, "Well, Doc, every night before I go to bed I have a little puff of opium. It gives me a nice night's sleep and doesn't make me feel dopey in the morning."

Bang went my Sunday-school lesson, as all the students started to laugh.

Despite that bad experience, I'm going to recommend some things that you can do to have a healthier old age. Old people are so careless about keeping their bodies in decent order, but if the body's on the blink, it certainly makes enjoying your old age very difficult.

The most obvious way to keep yourself in good shape is exercise. Some people who are very self-disciplined do their exercises at home — push-ups and so on — which is a good

idea, although it doesn't appeal to me. A very simple thing
that I like to do is walk as much as possible. In our society
it's so easy just to take the car every time we go out. "After
all, we're going to the shopping mall, and we're going to
bring back some very heavy things." Well, *walk* and carry
the ten-pound bag of potatoes or whatever you're buying.
You'll be better off for it. But you have to walk with a purpose, not just saunter. I walk until I feel a little tightness in
the chest, though I'm careful not to overdo it.

Swimming is good exercise, too. Just be sure to do *something*. And whatever you do, don't just sit around watching
television. That's an absolutely poisonous habit. You may
have to rely on TV some day, but put it off as long as you
can.

Avoiding overeating is another plus. I like to tuck in once
in a while, but otherwise I try to avoid overindulgence, because an older person who's overweight is really in trouble.

It's just as important to exercise the mind. Keep your
mind alert by staying in touch with current events, taking
university courses, studying a new subject. I've gone back to
studying high school mathematics. I have some textbooks,
and I spend two or three hours a week going over them. As
Wilder Penfield used to explain, all of these areas of knowledge have their own paths in your brain. If you don't use
those paths, it's just the same as a rain forest — they get
overgrown. It's tragic when you meet some older people and
can almost watch the weeds growing over their paths. Because of that mental laziness, they become inflexible. They
get an arthritis of the brain, which prevents them from ex-
ploring or adapting to new ideas. "Oh, it's new, and I have
no use for it," they say. "The world's all going to hell anyway."

Many older people spend too much time reminiscing,
harping on some phase of their lives. Reminiscing isn't bad

in itself — but bring it up-to-date. Use it to better your life *now*. Get inspiration by thinking about some of the people you've influenced in your life or who've influenced you. Track them down and write them a letter. Go to reunions and find out what's happening to all your old friends *now*.

Another way to keep the mind working is to stay in touch with young people. Women feel a little differently about that, I think. My wife says, "I raised the kids, I've done my share," and I can understand that. But I do think it's important to keep up the communication between the generations. That's something we miss with so many older people being in institutions. Grandparents miss the stimulation of being with children, and the kids aren't exposed to the natural process of aging.

No matter how much you do to keep yourself physically and mentally fit, there are certain problems you simply won't be able to avoid. You have to plan for these. Aging isn't a disease, but the body *is* wearing out. The parts don't all wear out at the same time, just as in a car. Once I had a car with a perfectly good engine, but the body was rusted through. Another time the body was good, but the transmission went. You have to realize that in your particular case, depending on your genes and your experience, you may have certain problems to overcome. For instance, if you're starting to develop arthritis as you approach retirement, don't take piano lessons. If eye trouble runs in your family, it wouldn't be smart to become a stamp collector. It's all just common sense and good planning.

One of the limitations you have to face is that probably, eventually, you will no longer be able to live on your own. Someone recently suggested to a retired friend of mine whose wife had died that he might want to go into a retirement home. He really flew off the handle! "By golly," he said, "I raised five daughters. They got their education, everything they wanted. And now they're going to look after the old man. The hang with your institution!"

I'm wondering if that kind of revolt is going to take place all over Canada — because, in this country, we have really shucked off the responsibility of looking after our older people. We have about twice as many elderly people in institutions as Germany and Britain do, even though we have about the same living standard.

Originally there was no alternative to the family looking after the old folks, so Mama and Papa tried to have a lot of kids so that at least one would survive and look after them. (It still works that way today in many parts of the Third World.) Then the arrangement was that the daughter who didn't get married looked after the parents. By the time they died, it was probably too late for her to find a husband, so she inherited the house, and that was her security.

Then society became very mobile. People began looking to the government and the nursing home to help bear the burden. Maybe Mom and Pop lived in Ontario and the kids had moved to Vancouver and Halifax. Or everyone worked and no one had time to look after the parents. When they got old, you put them in a filing cabinet. You went to see them every week or two, but then they started to get confused — maybe it was Alzheimer's, or maybe it was just the effect of living in an institution — and they didn't know who you were, so you only went once in a while and on special occasions. The grandchildren were bored stiff. The old folks didn't talk sense anyway, and the kids lost all respect for them. That's not a healthy way for a family to end up.

I think the pendulum has swung too far. If only for the sake of our consciences, the family is going to have to take more responsibility in future because the institution is a less-than-ideal way of looking after the aged. Although they are staffed by heroic people who are very loving and caring, they're still institutions. A friend of mine went into a nursing home recently. Up until the time he went in he had been an active man with a very alert mind. Within a few weeks, all he could talk about was what he had had for supper and the digestive tracts of himself and his table companions.

What has happened is that we are subcontracting the care of our older people to the government and to nursing homes. We have to get back to the idea that there is a family obligation. Many people say, "We have good nursing homes. Why the heck should we have to look after Grandma?" or, "We're not qualified to look after an old person." I agree that when you really are unqualified, then the government, the health services, the nursing homes, should all be ready to help you. Everything that modern science can offer should be available, irrespective of whether or not you can pay for it. But it's *your* job.

But, of course, times have changed. In Canada, families are scattered. The extended family has broken down. Frequently both the men and the women in the family go out to work. Having Grandpa move into the back bedroom just may not be possible so we have to look for alternatives.

The Chinese have similar problems and have found some very pragmatic solutions. With their low standard of living they can't afford to live wastefully so they pool their resources. Children who know that they're not going to be able to look after their parents will get together with other young people in the same situation and persuade their parents to share a house, perhaps with a younger couple to help them out.

We could try the same kind of solution here — in fact, many people already have. Although it's good to see that she's managed to stay out of an institution, why should one old lady live by herself in a four-bedroom house? It's lonely; it's probably not healthy; it doesn't make economic sense;

and if she's living in a large metropolitan area, it may not even be safe. If there are four old ladies in that situation, perhaps three out of the four should sell their houses and live together, even though it may not be easy for them to adapt to each other. Perhaps they could fix up a basement apartment and have a young couple live there rent-free in return for looking after the place, doing the shopping, maybe getting the evening meal.

However, when you make that kind of suggestion, people in our society tend to say, "It's none of your damn business!" We have a false sense of independence. Just because you are financially independent doesn't mean you're psychologically independent. We all need other people. Older people will have to learn to become interdependent, to forget about their individual rights and find pragmatic solutions if they want to stay out of the old folks' home.

We faced this problem with Amy's father. She had planned to come out to China so that we could get married, but her father, who was a widower, had lost his right arm and required a great deal of attention. In those days there were few nursing homes, the pension scheme wasn't very generous, and he hadn't been able to save up much for his retirement. It never occurred to anybody that anyone but Amy would look after him.

So Mr. Hislop came to China. In those days it was a wild, bandit-filled country. Mr. Hislop, who was in his seventies, had scarcely ever been out of Whitby, but he enjoyed China and he was never scared. He travelled in a boxcar, with no toilet facilities except a couple of boards knocked out of the floor, men at one end, women at the other. He kept saying, "Boy, won't I have something to tell the boys around the stove in the wintertime!"

He collected a tremendous number of tales in the year he was with us. He loved to see the wounded bandits brought in. We'd take the guns away and store them in a walk-in cupboard with a cement lining and a double-steel door. When the bandits had recovered, we'd hand the guns back and give them a twenty-four-hour start before we let anyone know they'd been released. Mr. Hislop always came to see them leave and speculated whether they'd make it to the hills before they were caught.

He was a unique figure because, at that time, there were no old Chinese — they just didn't survive to that age. The Chinese had a deep and sincere reverence for old people, so he could wander wherever he liked without the slightest danger. If he was limping a bit after a long walk, a couple of Chinese would get under each arm and help him back to the compound. A farmer would put down his hoe and walk with him for a little while, then go back to work.

Eventually Amy's sister, who had been out of the country, returned to Canada, and Mr. Hislop went back to live with her. Three years later he died of a stroke. That was back in the Twenties. I suppose if that situation came up today, he would probably have gone into a retirement home. People would think we were terrible kids if we took him out to such a wild and dangerous place. Yet, in many ways, it was an ideal retirement.

8

Learning How to Die

When I was working as a doctor, I got quite a reputation as a plug puller. That accusation never bothered me a bit, and I hope whoever is looking after me when I reach that stage is just as hard-boiled.

It wasn't until I got to Borneo in 1971 that I had the fancy equipment to keep someone alive artificially. We had an elderly patient in the hospital there who had had a stroke. We just couldn't get his blood pressure down. He'd had strokes before, and it was obvious he would keep having them, one after the other. We had him in the oxygen tent, unconscious and hooked up to the intravenous and various other machines and monitors. Then his best friend and his family came in to see him. Like most of the Iban tribal people, they were primitive, but they had terrific horse sense. "Is this all that's left of Dad?" they asked. "Isn't there anything you can do for him?" I explained that we could keep him going with the machinery, but he would never leave the hospital and he might never be conscious again. "That's crazy," they said. "Cut off those machines at once." So I disconnected the oxygen bottle and pulled the plug of the respirator, and the old man died not long after.

Every time a similar situation came up, the family of the patient made the same decision. They were willing to make that decision, because they were determined not to deprive the next generation by spending effort and money on prolonging the existence of the previous generation. So it was no sin to pull the plug. In fact, they thought that, as the doctor, that was part of my job. And it didn't bother me to do it. I felt I was doing a charitable thing.

The Iban people were primitive, yet they were very sensible and very unsentimental about death. It surprises me that a sophisticated, educated society like our own seems so incapable of dealing with death. We're very indecisive about letting death happen naturally. Perhaps in the back of our minds somewhere we believe that if we spend enough money, we can bring back Mom or Dad or Aunt Mary. We don't want to recognize that there's a time when a person has to say goodbye and go on across the river. What's happened to us that we can't deal frankly and sensibly with death anymore?

The whole issue of plug-pulling was clarified for me a few years ago at a national conference in Winnipeg on terminal illness and palliative care. A young gerontologist there explained that there are three kinds of death. When we hitch up an electrocardiogram and find the needle's not moving, we say that person is "cardiac dead." If we stick the electrodes on the scalp and the needle's still not moving, we call that "cerebral death." But there's a third kind of death — "social death." That's the person who has gone downhill steadily and for weeks has not been able to recognize even his or her nearest relative. You know the patient is not going to recover. What you see is not your father or mother or friend. That person died some months ago. The body is there, the heart is beating, the kidneys are functioning, but that's not life — that's just a body.

That idea helps me to deal with some very tragic cases, intimate friends of ours who have been in that state for many years. It's ridiculous to me to think that those bodies are Beatrice or Margaret. They used those bodies for many years, but now their souls have passed on.

Because so much of my experience has been in the Third World, I feel much more keenly about this business of keeping bodies alive. I'm afraid that if you use money for treating the hopeless, you may be cheating the hopeful. According to UNICEF, 40,000 children under three years of age are dying every twenty-four hours from malnutrition and preventable disease. For only five dollars each, those children could be immunized against disease. Most of their other health problems are very simple and cheap to solve. Yet it has cost $50,000 a year to keep one of my friends alive for the last six years. Three hundred thousand dollars could have kept alive hundreds of babies in the places I've worked.

The big question is, What's the boundary between active and passive euthanasia? What's the difference between letting someone slip away naturally and actually interfering so that they die earlier? Are there times when it's acceptable to help people die rather than face great pain and loss of dignity? These are all difficult questions that nobody has any easy answers for.

Several times a friend of mine asked me to help him die. He was suffering from an incurable disease. He didn't enjoy life. There was nothing left for him, he said, but boredom, at best, and pain and resentment, at worst. I had to refuse, but I know that I would think it a blessing if I were in that state and someone acceded to my request.

Eventually we did "pull the plug" on my friend, and he died quite peacefully the next day. I was able to tell the doctor that he had requested that no artificial means be used to keep him alive, and the family backed me up. Fortunately, we had a sympathetic doctor, but I think doctors are often afraid that if the patient dies, they'll be accused of not extending themselves. In some cases I think the doctor is waiting for the family to make a decision, while the family is waiting for the doctor to say something. It's like the old-style polite Chinese; you couldn't get them out the garden gate because they were so busy bowing, each insisting that the other go first.

I think our attitudes have been changed a great deal by such people as Henry Pitney Van Dusen, the prominent theologian at Union Theological Seminary in New York. He and his wife were both facing a painful, debilitated old age: he had had a stroke and she had severe arthritis. One day they sat down in the kitchen, wrote their farewell notes together, then took an overdose of sleeping pills.

To me this is a different situation from one in which a severely depressed person commits suicide. It was a conscious, well-thought-out choice, and everyone should have the right to make that choice. I hope we're reaching a stage in which a person could leave a living will, asking that his life not be sustained by artificial means, even that he be allowed to commit suicide, if it seems appropriate.

Whatever we decide, obviously no doctor should have to take the sole responsibility for ending the patient's life. Probably the best solution would be to form a committee at each hospital, consisting of a doctor, a clergyperson and a psychiatrist. The person who is dying or the relatives of that person could appeal to the committee asking that the sick person be allowed to die and even be assisted to die.

I hope we're not far away from that kind of solution, but I also recognize that in our Western society we have trouble dealing with death itself. We have a lot of inhibitions in talking about death, just as we have inhibitions about discussing sex. Funeral directors tell us that people who have everything else well lined up have made no preparations at all for their funerals, as if they were going to live forever. Even when they're seriously ill, people in our society don't like to face the fact of death until the doctor puts down the stethoscope and it's too late.

I learned so much about dealing with death when I lived among the Muslims. My patients were Palestinian Arabs, living in the Gaza Strip, a tiny area surrounded by a barbed wire fence. Eighty percent of them were refugees who had lost everything in life and had no compensation. In such a small community, we became very close to our patients, and I was often with them when they died. The equanimity I saw was something I admired and valued very deeply.

The case I remember most clearly was a man of seventy-four who had been going steadily downhill for about a month. It was only a few days before he died that we discovered he had a son in Oxford. The family asked if they should send for him, and I replied, "I doubt if he'll get here on time, but by all means send for him."

I was going to see the father about four or five times a day, and each evening when I had finished my rounds, I would have a long chat with him. Then one Sunday morning they called to tell me he was dying. I was with him for about two hours. Unlike most people who are dying, he was very clear-minded right up to within ten minutes before he passed away. He asked me to hold his hand and said, "I feel very peaceful." Instead of showing any feelings of resentment, he would keep repeating, "Allah has been very good to me." It was more than just a shibboleth; he really meant it. When he finally died, it was with a spirit of thanksgiving and complete trust.

When he was gone, I came out of the room to find his family. For the first time I met the son from Oxford, a very handsome, tall gentleman. I was quite intimidated because I thought he might blame me for his father's death. He might ask, "Why didn't you let me know a month ago, and I could have taken Dad to the medical centre in Oxford, where the facilities are so much better and he could have been saved." He stepped forward and raised his hand. I thought he was going to hit me, but instead he shook my hand and said, "We are so grateful that Allah chose you to be the last one to be with Dad. No doctor likes to lose a patient. But we appreciate so much what you have done for our father." I've never had as warm a gesture of thanks in those circumstances from any Christian family.

I believe the Muslim passes over more smoothly because he has developed an awareness throughout his life of constantly living in God's presence. He uses God's name every third or fourth sentence. He's going to do something "if God wills." If something nice happens to him, he doesn't shrug his shoulders and say, "I was lucky." He says, "God was good to me." A person who lives with that attitude is obviously going to face death very differently from a person whose religion was emphasized only on Sundays.

I also noticed that the families were usually very calm. Death was inevitable; it was Allah's will. Relatives would ask openly about it, and you could talk to them sensibly. When you told them the prospects weren't good, all they'd say was, "Allah is merciful." They would go home, gather the family around, explain exactly what was happening and begin to make plans. All of this was done openly and freely, without any recrimination or false hope. They just didn't seem to worry unduly about death. I suppose if you didn't

like the Muslims, you called it fatalism. If you did like them,
you called it a tremendous faith. That's what I called it, and
it was wonderful to see.

Another group that seemed to deal well with death were
the native people I met when I was working at Fort Simpson
in 1978. I was looking after a man named Alfred. He'd been
an alcoholic, which had mucked up his heart, but in the
past ten years he'd lived a virtuous life. Now his heart was
tired, and he knew he wasn't going to make it. One night
some of his old pals were visiting him in the hospital. As
they were leaving, he roused himself and said, "Goodnight,
fellas. I'll see you in the morning on the other side of the river." Then he fell back on the bed and died about three hours
later. It was one of my most vivid experiences of death and a
model for me of someone who was able to face his end without fear. Alfie was a Christian, but I think a lot of his attitude came from his native heritage.

We need beliefs that can fit us for death as well as for life.
So I believe that we should be adapting some of the Muslim
and native teachings to our own religious instruction — particularly now that we have so many people reaching old age.

I'm sure that many old people are thinking about death.
In fact, many are thinking very negatively. Certainly those
who are counselling seniors in our country should talk with
them about it so seniors can meet death with greater equanimity. But we need to begin with younger people. I may be
considered morbid for suggesting it, but we should also
make classes on death part of our school curriculum. It's going to happen to everybody, after all, so why not prepare a
person's mind for it? It would only take two or three hours
spread over a student's time in high school, and it might
help us escape the tremendous fear we feel about death.

I remember one old Chinese friend who certainly had the
right kind of philosophy, although he had resisted any

Christian influence. Like most classical Chinese scholars, he was about eighty percent sure that when he died that would be the end of it.

One time I dropped in on him to talk about a land deal. He took me back to his very orderly but rather sparsely furnished sitting room — just two black chairs and a table with a marble top. We were having our tea when to my surprise he said, "I must show you my coffin." And there, in a dark corner, was a huge, heavy coffin with a beautiful red-lacquered lid. I went over to admire it. He explained that he was getting on and felt he should make the proper preparations. He asked me to give him a hand, and we lifted the top off. And then, to my horror, he crawled into it! "Look at this," he said. "Isn't it marvellous?" He looked all ready to be a corpse. All you had to do was stick a lily in his hands and start reading the burial service. He was cheerful and excited. "Isn't it nice that it fits around the shoulders?" he said, as if he was trying on a new suit.

It was quite an inspiration to me that he had the kind of philosophy that would enable him to face the inevitable so cheerfully. I was having to face the inevitable myself on a regular basis. Those were troubled times in China. I walked by my predecessor's grave every day. He'd been shot by bandits, and I was dealing with an average of one gunshot wound every day for sixteen years. The idea that I might be shot was never far from my mind.

I learned something interesting from that situation. People who have to learn to face up to death don't get depressed about it. In fact, the opposite happens. There's a release, a new freedom: once you've learned to live with the idea of your own death, it's one thing you don't have to be afraid of anymore.

Many people, even under normal conditions, learn to live with the knowledge that death is close at hand — fishermen, miners, police and soldiers have to cope with the risks of their jobs. Anyone who's ever had an operation under general anesthetic has to acknowledge that he may die. Everybody has to face death at some time, and there's no reason why it shouldn't be faced, no reason why you should get excited about death. There's a tremendous psychological release when you say to yourself, "Yes, I have to face this."

This is where I disagree strenuously with how some doctors deal with their patients. I have worked with female cancer patients twice — once with some very able people in England and then later for five months in Sweden. Doctors in the two countries had entirely different approaches. At that time in England you never told the patient she had cancer. Even if she asked, you'd lie right in her face: "No, you have a lesion that might develop into cancer if we don't treat it." I'd ask the doctors, "Can't you tell the patient the truth?" They'd say, "Oh, no, we can't do that. Why add a mental disease to what is already a very serious physical disease? She'll just worry if you tell her she has cancer." What they failed to realize, of course, was that the patient had already guessed and wished that someone would tell her the truth.

In Sweden, however, as soon as the cancer was diagnosed, you called in the patient and her relatives and talked about the situation. You showed them the statistics. You told the patient, "You have grade two cancer of the cervix, and we're going to treat you. You have a sixty-eight percent chance of being alive at the end of five years." If you were afraid the patient would have emotional problems dealing with the illness, then you would get her some therapy. Ever since that experience, I've used the Swedish approach. If the sick person cannot get the truth from her doctor, then to whom can she turn? Whether you're dealing with cancer or AIDS or some other life-threatening disease, the doctor owes it to the patient to tell him or her the truth, because facing up to death at least gives one a chance to deal with one's fears.

Of all the people I've known, there is one in particular who impressed me by the way he was able to handle that fear of death. Donald Hankey was an English doctor who worked with our ambulance unit during the war. No matter how dangerous the situation, he seemed to be totally without fear.

One Easter weekend in 1938 Hankey and another colleague, Bruce Copland, and I were travelling across the lines together. We had been trying to negotiate an agreement between the Japanese and the Chinese guerrillas so that the Japanese could get their wounded out in exchange for the release of their Chinese prisoners.

Everything had gone well that day. We were riding our bicycles back along the dikes, and we could see the lights of our mission compound. We were almost home. Suddenly a Japanese sentry jumped up in front of us and yelled, "Halt!" He was a short fellow, but he made up for it by having a long rifle and a very long bayonet. He stuck the bayonet right against Hankey's stomach and started jabbering away in Japanese, almost paralysed with fear.

We had brought Bruce Copland along because he spoke a few words of Japanese, but all he could remember was French, and he started speaking that. Meanwhile, the sentry was still shouting, and his bayonet was shaking alarmingly. But Hankey was the completely unflappable Englishman. He reached out and steadied the sentry's bayonet, then turned to Bruce. "Please speak to this man, Mr. Copland," he said. "He seems to be nervous." Finally Copland was able to choke out an explanation in Japanese, and the sentry allowed us to pass safely into the mission compound.

Our group would often discuss why it was that the rest of us got terribly frightened but Hankey seemed to be without fear. He had such a simple explanation for it. "After all," he used to say, "if you've never done anything wrong to any-body in your life, then you have nothing to be afraid of."

That made me realize that part of our fear of death is that we will leave something undone that we should have done. If you can face danger with a clear conscience, you don't feel the same fear. When he was about ninety-eight or ninety-nine, my dad used to tell Amy sometimes, "You know, if this is the day I'm going to go, that's okay. I'm ready. All the accounts have been straightened out." And that removed his fear of death.

I think this attitude can be cultivated. If you have an en-mity with someone — perhaps someone in your family, per-haps a son or daughter who rebelled — see if you can straighten that out. And if you do, then perhaps you can face the possibility of dying with greater serenity.

Although we need to learn to face death, a healthy fear of it is also a necessary thing. You wouldn't want a teenager who was learning to drive a car not to have a fear of dying! In wartime we had to learn to strike that delicate balance between fear and acceptance of death. Donald Hankey died later in the war when he was inoculating troops against ty-phus fever. He caught typhus because he had forgotten to inoculate himself! Perhaps it was that admirable fearless-ness that killed him. We had to conquer that fear or we were no good to anybody; but, at the same time, we had to take all the precautions we could reasonably take.

For the doctors, this often led to ethical dilemmas. We all carried about twenty-five or thirty tablets of sulfa and a nee-dle loaded with a double dose of morphine, enough to knock out a horse. We usually carried this in a little tin box. We also carried a dressing, which had great mythical value. You could moisten it with a bit of water, or even urine, and it would give off chlorine. (We called it the "damn-fool ban-dage" because even a doctor couldn't put it on wrong.) The theory was that if you got hit, you would take the sulfa, give yourself a shot of morphine, put on the bandage, and this would keep you alive. It gave us a great feeling of assurance to have it, to know that at least we had a sporting chance. But when we were surrounded by wounded people, it was difficult to resist the temptation to use it for one of them. On the other hand, it wouldn't have helped more than one person, and then there was an increased risk that the doctor would be put out of action, so I kept the supplies for myself. Fortunately, I never had to use them.

Norman Bethune made a different decision than I did, and that's the real reason he died. He punctured his finger on the razor-sharp edge of a rib during an operation. Later, when the finger got infected, his Chinese assistant said, "I think it's time for your 'tin can,' doctor." Bethune didn't have it. He'd used his medication on one of the soldiers. It was an heroic thing to do, and it cost him his life.

Because death was constantly present during those war years, we had to learn to deal with it. This isn't true in our modern Western society. In fact, we are unnaturally cut off from death, as if it was something obscene that we shouldn't talk about. In earlier times we were forced to deal with death. During the great plagues, there wasn't a family who didn't lose at least one person. Even a hundred years ago, almost everyone had a little brother or sister who had died. Today there are very few deaths at home. The image of the whole family standing around while Papa passes on is a false one. More likely, Papa died in hospital at 2 A.M. and the family didn't know about it until the phone rang at 7. There might have been a nurse in the room when he died. Or there might not.

The fact that we're so cut off from death makes it difficult for us to grieve properly. Rural Canada handled it much better in the old days. The bereaved person was surrounded by friends. Everybody helped out. Even in wartime, women were comforted because the grief was shared. A woman might lose her son, but down the street there was someone else whose son had been killed, and around the corner was another mother whose son had come back blind.

I wonder how many people a widowed spouse or grieving parent has to confide in today? We're all so busy. The funeral only lasts thirty minutes. Then everyone has a cup of tea, and that's it. After the first twenty-four hours, people start to avoid the bereaved person because she's grieving — they don't want to disturb her. Actually, that's the time when she most needs fellowship and support. Instead, the widow goes home alone to her big empty house, and there are Bill's clothes hanging in the cupboard — and they may still be there three years later. I've been in a house where Mother's room is still exactly as she left it, with her hairbrush on the dresser. That's a very serious problem. It means the person did not do his or her grieving and then recover from it. It's psychologically unhealthy, even psychopathic, to carry grief to such an extent.

I remember being shocked to see a widow in Zaire rolling around on the ground, screaming, for nearly eight hours. Finally some of the relatives comforted her and took her home. I suggested to them that I should give her a sedative, but they said, "Don't worry. We'll have a big feast tonight. She'll be all right." The next morning she came in to the hospital to pick up her husband's clothes, and she was quite cheerful. I had the feeling she was open for applications to take his place. Apparently she had gotten great relief from expressing her grief with vigor for eight hours, and then it was over. Her grief had been worked out, with the support of her relatives, and now she was ready to go on with her life.

We show grief in our society through funerals, but our attitude to them isn't always healthy. By Muslim standards, the tremendous amount of money we spend on our funerals is, frankly, obscene. We have this idea that if we really loved the person, we'll be willing to spend a few extra thousand on the funeral — which is a crass way of looking at things.

In the Muslim community where I lived, even the wealthiest person in town was simply stripped naked, washed, wrapped in a sheet and placed in a coffin with a trapdoor. The coffin was carried through the streets and then suspended over the grave while somebody pulled the string, and the body dropped into the grave. The body was covered over, and the coffin went back to the shop for the next time it was needed. It fitted so well with our Christian Gospel, which tells us that when we get to the end, we're all the same in God's eyes.

The Indians also seemed to be compelled to show how much they cared for the deceased, but they had a different way of showing it. When I went to India, I was told I'd have to get a lawyer for the hospital. I couldn't figure out what we'd need a lawyer for. Nobody had anything against the hospital. We payed our accounts on time. We were a charitable hospital, so if anyone couldn't pay, we didn't sue them. What would we need a lawyer for? But the British had bequeathed a beautiful legal system to India. There were so many law courts waiting to be used and so many judges and lawyers eager to be employed. So one of the ways you could show your great love for the deceased was to launch a lawsuit against the doctor who last looked after him.

In no time at all our surgical practice had not one lawsuit but three! We engaged the best lawyer in town, a teacher at the law faculty of the local arts college, and gave him a twenty-five-rupee retaining fee, which was worth about twenty-five dollars, and about five rupees for each court appearance. Nothing was ever settled in court, of course. Every time we went, the case was adjourned. They had lost some of the evidence or the key witness was not available that day so the hearing was postponed — not for a week but for six months. So the case went on and on. Every Saturday afternoon I'd go to the Rotary meeting, and the standard greeting would be, "How's your case doing?" Everyone had a lawsuit of some type going, and we were all deeply interested in each other's cases. I'm sure that when I left India, there were still several outstanding suits against me.

The main point of all this, of course, was that the family must really have loved the deceased. They cared so much about him that they'd sued the hospital for 5,000 rupees. It doesn't make much more sense than spending thousands of dollars on a solid oak casket that's never going to be seen again. When you get down to it, grief really is a form of selfishness. It's *my* life that's been upset. It's *my* loneliness that has been increased. *I've* been deprived of this important relationship. What we have to learn to do is face death — whether it's our own or someone else's — do our grieving, and then get on with our lives.

Recently a family I know handled a death in a very healthy and moving manner. The mother was dying of cancer. Her husband brought her home from the hospital about a week before she died. He looked after her in her last hours. When she was gone, the family undressed the body, washed it and fixed it up for the coffin. All the kids took part. They got rid of all the mysticism and superstition surrounding death and faced it very realistically. Like the gerontologist in Winnipeg, they were saying, "That was Mother, but now she's gone. This is the body she used and that's all it is, so don't be sentimental about it. Now we're going to get it ready for burial. And then we'll look to the future."

9

The Kind of Christian
I Am

Even though I was a missionary for forty-seven years and was the leader of a major Protestant denomination, there are some people who would say that technically I'm not a Christian. Because of my upbringing and experience, I don't believe a lot of the doctrines Christians traditionally believe. Let me tell you how that happened and why I think it's okay.

In 1912 my mother left China, taking my older sisters home to North America to get their education, so my Dad and I were on our own together for the next three years. Although he was very busy at the hospital, Dad always made time for me on Sundays. In the afternoon we'd read together — the books were usually way over my head, but Dad thought I ought to read them. Then we'd go out for a walk and discuss them. From those conversations with Dad I got the powerful idea that God was a God of love. I never had the notion that God was a punishing God. My father resented that idea, and it set him apart from the more conservative, evangelistic missionaries who were preaching to the Chinese.

When these missionaries were going on about the terrifying things God might do to sinful people, Dad would say to
me, "Now don't let them bother you. That's their idea, and
you have your own idea of what God's like." (In fact, the
conservative gospel was probably better suited to the situation. The Chinese could understand a god who was good to
you if you were good, but if you were bad, boy, he would certainly let you have it!)

Dad could never pass on to the Chinese anything he himself didn't believe. Sometimes his medical assistants would
ask him, just as the disciples asked Jesus, "Why is this man
crippled? Was it his sin or his parents' sin that made him
this way?" And Dad would answer them that God was a
God of love — we didn't know why these things happened
to people, but they weren't meant as punishments, and it
was our job to try to correct them. Otherwise, every time you
healed someone, you were thwarting God's condemnation
of that person.

When Dad and I read the Bible together, he made it clear
that the Old Testament was not a textbook about history or
how the world was created. It was the religious mythology of
the Hebrew people. Although it had an important message,
it wasn't literal fact.

So by the time I was in my early twenties, studying medicine in Toronto, I found that I didn't believe many of the
doctrines most Christians believed. The Virgin Birth and
the Resurrection were the two main hitches. As a medical
person, I just couldn't accept these events as fact. That
worried me, so I went to see Dr. Pidgeon at Bloor Street
Presbyterian Church. After I had explained my problem, he
said, "Bob, you have to find your own ideas about God and
not let other people form your religion for you. If something
doesn't make sense to you, then don't accept it. The Christian religion should appeal to a person's common sense."

Dr. Pidgeon's words helped me greatly, and since that time I've never worried about having unorthodox beliefs or about changing my beliefs when someone presents me with a better idea.

One area where I'm inclined to be heretical is the miraculous. As a doctor, I've never believed much in miracles. Many of the miraculous healings in the Bible can be explained in medical terms. For example, psoriasis has often been misdiagnosed as leprosy, and there's a very heavy psychological factor in psoriasis. If you remove stress from the patient, the disease will often miraculously clear up in a number of days. Some of the lepers who were healed in the Bible may actually have been suffering from psoriasis.

In India I would sometimes see a person with a useless leg. There was nothing actually wrong with the leg, but years ago the person had decided, perhaps because of some religious idea, that that limb was going to be paralysed. He had curled it up, and after ten or fifteen years of non-use it was a pretty useless limb. Yet the nerves, the bones and the muscles were there. The psychology of society in Jesus' time would have been quite similar to India's, I think, so he may have "healed" some similar cases.

On the other hand, I have lived in a time when, in the scientific world, many miracles have happened — penicillin, insulin, inoculation — and I know that there are miracles in healing. Anybody who's dealt with cancer has had those cases where one actually sees the cancer cells under the microscope, one knows the treatment wasn't particularly effective, yet ten years later the patient is still alive and hasn't had any recurrence of the cancer.

I have also known people who claimed to have experienced miracles. I met one in China, just after V-J Day. Our ambulance unit was stationed at Zhengzhou, doing relief and rehabilitation work. We shared an old Baptist mission compound with about 500 Japanese who were patiently waiting to surrender. Despite the war — and despite the fact that the Japanese all had nice warm winter uniforms while we were freezing in summer clothes! — we all got on well.

One cold, dark night just before Christmas, a dust storm was blowing out of Mongolia, and we were all huddled around the fire. Suddenly there was a knock at the door. There stood a tiny American lady, bundled in a tattered, blue, quilted coat. "Is the war really over?" she whispered.

Helen Bailey had been one of three Baptist missionaries who were working with the local people along the Yellow River. When the other two ladies fled from the Japanese, Miss Pay Lee, as she was known, had stayed behind. In 1938 her territory was engulfed by the Japanese army, and all contact with her was lost. We assumed she had been captured and killed. But now here she was, bedraggled, but obviously alive. She was hesitant to enter our house because "boys and girls were living together," and she assumed a considerable degree of "sin" must be going on. But eventually we got her to come in and cleaned her up, and she began to tell her story.

For the entire eight years she had depended entirely on her Christian converts to support, shelter, clothe and feed her. In the best of times these people were among the poorest in China, and for three years they had suffered through one of the worst man-made famines in history, yet they had always been able to spare her something. The Japanese had offered thousands of dollars for her capture, but no one had ever given her away, even under torture. That she survived at all was miraculous.

A few days later we held a Christmas Eve party for our Japanese neighbors. When Miss Bailey entered and was introduced, their eyes nearly popped out of their heads! Was this *the* Pay Lee, who had eluded capture for so many years?

For a long time they had assigned an entire cavalry unit to look for her. Helen Bailey assured them that indeed she was that mythical character and told them about the time they had nearly captured her. She knew that a search party was close at hand so she had been hiding out in some caves beside the river. One morning she awoke at dawn to see a man in luminous white robes standing in the doorway of the cave. "Helen, hurry and go west," the angel said. "Now! Hurry!" In the early dawn she quickly rolled up her blanket and few possessions and walked to the west as fast as she could. About fifteen minutes later she heard a Japanese search party come to her cave, throw in hand grenades and then go in with flame throwers.

The Japanese were totally baffled. "This 'angel,' " they asked. "What is it?" Did it have wings? Was it RAF or U.S. Air Force? Did it have a radio? Had there been some behind-the-lines unit at work that Japanese intelligence knew nothing about? Miss Bailey just said, "Oh, you wouldn't understand."

I have to admit that, like those Japanese officers, there are many things in life that I don't understand. I wouldn't dare say there are *no* miracles. It's very possible that Miss Pay Lee's angel really did appear, but I think God works mainly through people, and I wouldn't want to depend on miracles too much. Still, there are many things I can't explain, and if someone wants to call them miracles, that's fine with me.

I suppose the biggest "miracle" that gives me trouble is the Resurrection. I don't believe that, in order for Jesus' teachings to survive, it was necessary for him to have a miraculous Resurrection. The ideas of many people — Socrates, Plato, Aristotle, various mathematicians and scientists — are embedded in our culture and philosophy of life. In India you might just as well say Gandhi didn't die, because like Jesus', his spirit has lived on in millions of people.

Gandhi's will was written on a little slip of paper that was found in his room, near his Bible, which was always open at the Sermon on the Mount. It read: "So long as my faith burns bright, as I hope it will, even if I stand alone, I shall be alive in the grave and, what is more, speaking from it."

That is what I call resurrection — that Jesus left so much in his three years of ministry that even though he wrote nothing down, even though his life was terminated, not only his disciples but hundreds of other people carried on his mission.

Similarly, I think those who know Jesus' message and have a vision of what he was trying to tell people, yet don't pass it on, are the ones who continue to obliterate him. Anyone who is hypocritical in his Christian life is helping to obliterate Christ just as much as the Roman soldiers did.

I don't like to think of Jesus as being superhuman. To me his message loses its impact if we put too much of the divine in him. My idea is that he was *human* and yet was able to portray a God of *infinite* love. The life of Jesus is a much more vital lesson when I look on it in that light than if he was a magician who could do miracles. He referred to himself as the Son of Man, and the seed of that divinity, I think, is in every human being. How much that seed is allowed to develop is our business. That is the secret of our humanity, what separates us from the finest of the animals.

In fact, I think this is the true story of creation — the way in which the Holy Spirit worked through evolution to bring about that bit of the divine in humanity. It was the spirit of God that got into the one-celled animals and showed them that by two or three combining, and then hundreds combining, they could begin to specialize. And, similarly, the lack of that spirit of adaptation and accommodation and struggle to improve exterminated certain branches of the animal kingdom. When we evolved from the best of the primates and finally crossed the boundary where we became human, that also was God working in us. And you still see the Holy Spirit working in people, no matter what their religion, to change history for the better. To me this is a much more fascinating story than Adam and Eve in the Garden.

As for the idea that Jesus' death is an atonement, I can't imagine a God who demanded that his beloved son should die for our sins. I think, rather, that Jesus died to show that you must *not* give up on your ideals, no matter how great the persecution, even at the expense of your life. You can tell from reading his words that he knew from the beginning that at some point he was going to collide with the Roman authorities, that they were going to try to wipe him out. That's why he kept telling his disciples, "I won't be here. You'll have to carry on. You'll have to stand by these ideals."

Because I don't accept the traditional doctrine that Jesus died to save us from our sins, Communion has a different meaning for me. I don't like the idea of eating Christ's body and drinking his blood. I think this practice is probably related to the primitive idea of tribal peoples that by eating the organs of your most heroic enemies you could graft into your system some of their courage. To me, that's absolutely repulsive. Yet there have been times when communion meant a great deal to me.

One Sunday morning during the war I went out with a few of the others from the ambulance unit to a communion service. The local deaconess, Judy Clark, had been given permission by the Anglican bishop to administer the sacraments. Ordinarily there were only about eight or ten people. But on this morning, thirty-two young boys, graduates of an Anglican boys' school on their way to air force training, had stopped for the service. It was a marvellous inspiration to join in the celebration and feel how important it was for them. They told us, "We feel this is the final blessing on our

Christian mission for our country." Just twenty-four hours
later the whole troop was wiped out in an air raid. Nevertheless, that communion ceremony was very important; we had
sealed a vow of fellowship at a time when there wasn't very
much else to hang on to.

I remember many other times during the war when things
were very sticky and people were about to launch out on a
job that they probably wouldn't come back from. We'd say,
"You're leaving tomorrow, so before you go, let's bring out
the food and the wine and have our last supper together.
Here's to our friendship over the years, and if this is the end,
at least we've been together, and we'll do this again to remember you." Having seen that in the barracks and the
mess hall among people who were going out to face death, I
think that's what Jesus was saying to his disciples: "Boys,
let's never forget this last time we're going to be together,
and here's to the time when we'll meet again on the other
side." To me, that's what communion really means. It's a
very solemn remembrance.

That's my collection of heresies. Probably, by the age of
twenty-two when I went to see Dr. Pidgeon about my
difficulties, I was really a Unitarian. What I *do* believe is
that there is one God, and Jesus is the supreme revelation of
that god, and the Holy Spirit is the power that came into
him and will come into anyone who wants to follow his
teachings. It comes to a greater degree in some and a lesser
degree in others. And it certainly can be cultivated, and it
certainly can be denied.

These are just *my* ideas, and I don't think there's anything
to be gained by confronting someone who has more conservative ideas. Certainly there are people who have *very* fun-
damentalist ideas, who because of their beliefs are able to
face martyrdom. Helen Bailey was a good example, but I've
met many more.

I remember a little Swedish missionary who lived a very precarious existence, distributing Bibles in Mongolia to wild tribal people. Like everyone else, she had a rifle slung across her saddle — and knew how to use it! She once impressed some bigtime American reporters by hitting a silver dollar at twenty feet with my pistol. Still, the Mongolians could easily have bumped her off, without any penalty, without anyone even knowing. However, she worked for years in those circumstances without losing her inspiration.

Another lady whose courage I admired was a colleague of Helen Bailey's. She had a boat and went up and down the Yellow River ministering to the people who worked on the ferries. After the war started, the other missionaries tried to convince her to leave. "As soon as the Japanese see your boat, they'll shoot you," we told her. "And when the air raids start, you'll be an obvious target."

But she had absolute faith that the Lord would protect her. "The text says, 'He will send angels with wings to guard over you,' " she told us. To which I replied, "Yeah, but the Japanese wings are out there now, and you have to watch out for them."

She lasted quite a while. The air raid pilots would go after her personally, puncturing her boat with machine-gun fire. She would just put corks in the holes. Then one day her goat was killed, and she realized that the Lord had a message for her. If the Lord couldn't protect her goat, then it was quite possible the Lord would fail to defend her. To our relief, she finally decided to leave.

I had a tremendous admiration for those people even though I couldn't disagree more with their theology, which I thought was *terrible*. They had a very narrow view — it wasn't enough to be a Christian; you had to be a Christian believing exactly as they believed. But perhaps that theology suited them. They certainly had an abundant faith.

I've learned that religious beliefs are a very private matter. What I believe wouldn't suit someone else, so I'm not going to try to propagate my ideas. I'll define my beliefs or defend them to anyone else who wants to know about them, but I'm not going to try to convert anyone to my ideas because I don't think they would fit someone else, any more than the shoes I wear or my dentures or my glasses would fit him. He hasn't had my experiences or training; he's had his own — and so he has to get his own philosophy of life.

I went to China as a missionary on a wave of religious enthusiasm following World War I, the war which was to "end all war and make the world safe for democracy." We were sent out to the mission fields under such slogans as "The evangelization of the world in this generation" or "By this sign conquer." We were the ones who had "The Light." Our attitude was a very good demonstration of the arrogance of Western culture.

Fortunately, I've had an excellent education since then, thanks to the many devout people I've met who didn't happen to be Christians. After associating with these people, I can never again think that they are all going to hell because they haven't been baptized and don't believe the same creed as I do. Many of the non-Christians I've met seem to have a very large chunk of what I would call the Holy Spirit — sometimes much more than some of our own people!

One time in India I took a trip with the governor of the Rotary district, a wealthy businessman who owned a cotton mill. We came to a temple that impressed him very much. There was a sunken spring with little ferns beside it. He turned to me and said, "This is the place for me to have a *dershan* — a vision. Will you excuse me for ten or fifteen minutes?" Then he went to sit beside the pool. There was no sound of prayers or hymns. When he came back, I could hardly believe my eyes. His face had that look that comes from very strong emotion — a sudden shock, terror, grief, great anger or a religious experience. "I had a marvellous vision," he said. It was as if, in the middle of discussing Rotary business, he had suddenly realized that this place demanded his devotion, and so he had put everything else aside and had been able to concentrate on being with the Eternal.

Another incident that particularly impressed me happened in the Middle East, when I went to Cairo to buy a second-hand car for our hospital in Gaza. I had to drive it back over about 160 miles of completely empty desert. Two Boy Scouts were supposed to accompany me, but they deserted at the last moment, and I was left to cross alone.

There was nothing but sand. Sometimes I could see the tarred road sticking out above the sand; other times it disappeared altogether beneath the sand and dust. I carried water and extra oil and gasoline, and every hour I stopped to check the car to make sure everything was all right, because if it had broken down, I would really have been in trouble.

About noon I stopped, got out my binoculars and looked around. There on the horizon, about a mile away, was a lone Arab nomad on his camel. The camel had stopped and kneeled down, and the nomad got off. I could see the flash of kerosene as he lit his little primus stove to make tea. Then he went around to the back of the camel, checked the sun to find the direction of Mecca, and began to say his prayers. I'm quite sure he couldn't see me. I was too far away, and he was probably almost blind from trachoma anyway, as so many of the desert nomads are. But although there was no one around to be impressed with his devotion, he went through the full Muslim prayers, kneeling, bowing, standing, kneeling again. This was his compact with God.

This incident, along with many other experiences with devout Muslims, gave me an idea of an ever-present God that I don't think Christians tend to have. When I was a little boy, sometimes I imagined God was spying on me, particularly if I was doing something I shouldn't have been doing. But from the Arab Muslim I got the idea that God was an invisible, loving power that was around you all the time. You didn't have to call on him; he was there anyway.

Once I came to respect people of other faiths, I no longer wanted to convert them to the same beliefs that I had. But what I would hope is that everybody could get a religious belief that's as useful for what he or she has to do in life as mine has turned out to be for what I had to do. Perhaps there are times when I as a Christian can share something I've learned, when I can show someone a helpful alternative. But often, I think, people don't understand our Christian message because we don't bother trying to understand their culture and beliefs.

That's why I admired so much the missionary work I saw being done in Borneo. The missionaries there studied the mythology, psychology and anthropology of the people. Their aim was, "How can we bring these people one step forward — not a giant step, just something that will improve their society and bring them a more wholesome attitude, while still retaining the many things that are so good in their way of life." In other words, the missionaries were promoting evolution rather than revolution. The tribal people weren't being converted; they were adapting the Christian religion to their own culture, taking what was best from both.

I saw a very successful example of this kind of mission work when I was in Taiwan, in the late 1920s. At that time the Japanese had colonized the country, and there were two Chinese brothers who were important figures in the Buddhist community. One was the editor of the leading newspaper, which was as critical as it could afford to be of the Japanese occupation. The other was the religious leader — you might call him the Buddhist archbishop. I knew his story because I often saw him at our hospital, where he was being treated for tuberculosis. He was a very enlightened, well-read man, and he was offended by some of the more enthusiastic missionaries, who were condemning the teachings of the Buddhist religion.

Then a missionary arrived who had studied the Buddhist religion for many years. In the National Library in Taipei there were forty-eight volumes of the Buddhist holy books, donated by the Empress Dowager of Japan, and Dr. Karl Reichelt could take any of those books and look up a reference just as easily as he could in his own Bible.

Dr. Reichelt met the archbishop and presented the teachings of Jesus in language and symbols that the Buddhist could understand. After a while, the archbishop said, "But that's what I believe in. In fact, you've said it better than it's said in any of our modern commentaries. I believe I may be following the teachings of Jesus more than I am following the teachings of Buddha." So the archbishop came to believe that he was a Christian. The way he explained it to me was to point at a little bottle of cough syrup on his window sill. "If I added enough water to fill that bottle up and then added a little bit more every day and still called it cough syrup, I'd be fooling myself," he said. "Literally, it would still be cough medicine. But it would get weaker and weaker. And eventually there would come a point when I'd have to call it water. It's the same with my religion. I'm becoming more and more a Christian, and I don't think I can call myself a Buddhist anymore."

The archbishop also felt that he had to announce his decision in the proper way so that his people would not feel hurt or betrayed, so he went to see his brother, the newspaper editor, and explained that he wanted to declare himself

a Christian. The brother confessed that since he had spoken
to Reichelt, he felt the same way. "But I haven't got the guts
to switch," he said. "It would ruin my paper, it would ruin
my career. It would mean changing my circle of friends and
starting all over again. But if you feel you should change, I
will help you."

A few days later, a death notice came out in the paper:
"Died this day, in the McKay Memorial Hospital, Our Rev-
erend Archbishop. . ." and so on, just as if he had physically passed away. The archbishop was very sick now and living in the hospital. I asked him what he would do next. "It's
very easy," he said. "We just put a birth notice in the paper,
and give me a Christian name — Paul or Peter or something like that." In fact, he lived only two more months.

This story shows that if you can explain Jesus' teaching in
terms of the ideas that someone already has about religion,
then the message will carry its own weight. And the onus to
do that is on us. At the same time we should try to learn
from the good things people of other religions already have.
And we need to learn a great deal, because one of the first
things a Muslim or Buddhist would discover on coming to a
so-called Christian country is that though Christianity may
have something to offer them, we Christians are not always
so hot on applying what's in our Good Book.

As a Christian, I know there are a lot of times when I've
been less than exemplary. I think to lead a truly Christian
life, I should be a lot more tolerant than I am. I'm sure I've
offended many people with my quick temper. There was
one doctor in India who had to be given a tranquillizer so
that he could stand to work with me. Usually when I've lost
my temper, my apologies have been accepted. But not always. One time in India when I was changing a young boy's
cast, he was making an unnecessary fuss. The parents were
complaining that I was too rough and implying that if I'd

been better qualified, the cast wouldn't have had to be changed in the first place. I lost my temper, and I was very sorry afterwards because the father was a medical colleague, and we were never able to be friends. I had embarrassed him in public, which in India was the unforgivable sin.

As a Christian, I also find there are situations that don't seem to have clear-cut solutions, and I sometimes wonder if I've made the right choices. For example, I wish that I could be as non-violent as Mr. Gandhi and his disciples. But there are times when I feel that one has to fight violence with violence. One time I caught a man trying to steal Red Cross supplies. He had a knife and seemed quite keen on using it. Some of the commandos I knew had taught me unarmed combat, so I went, as they say, for the jugular. It worked quite well. The thief dropped the knife and was paralysed for several hours after, but there was no permanent damage. I was quite delighted that my attack had worked, but I realized that officially that was not the proper solution. I don't know yet what the proper solution would have been in that situation. Deep down I know that through history, violence has never worked. But failure or confusion is no reason for giving up. We all fall short of the ideal that Jesus set, but we still try. When we're climbing that proverbial height, we may not get there. We may stumble, and at times we may slip right back to the bottom. But at least we're trying to climb higher.

No matter how inadequate Christians may often be, I still think Christianity has a lot to offer the non-Christian. Many people have the idea of an avenging God hanging over them. It's a tremendous relief to someone like that to realize, "No, I had a wrong idea of God. Actually God is a benevolent God who loves everybody. And whatever I do, I can still turn to God and he will love me." That idea of unlimited love can be a truly liberating force. But once you accept that

idea of Christian love, it changes your life. You'll begin to
realize that everything you have literally comes from God,
and the more you have, the greater your responsibilities. Jesus made this part of his gospel when he said, "From him to
whom much has been given, much will be required."

I met some young people who understood this when I was
asked to address the Mennonite Convention in St.
Catharines in 1974. A teenage girl in one of the seminars
told me that her group had been discussing how they should
be handling their money, how much they should be giving
to the church. I said, "You mean the tithe, the ten percent
that we're all supposed to give?" "Oh, no," she replied, "we
didn't discuss that. That already belongs to God. That goes
to him automatically. We were discussing what, as Christians, we should do with the rest of our money." I think if
you really believe in a loving God, like that girl, you see
yourself as the trustee of everything God has given you.

The Christian religion also emphasizes a universal God
— he's the God of everybody. This also is a very powerful
idea, especially in countries that have a rigid caste or class
system; it can completely change an individual's life.

One of the people I knew in India was a member of the
Bhil tribe, which is looked down on by the Indian people.
One day, when he was about ten or twelve, he was going
through the jungle and came across a missionary on horse-
back. The missionary asked the little boy if he could water
the horse in a nearby stream. "Oh, no," said the boy, who
knew that stream was poisoned by the vegetation around it.
"But I can lead you to a stream that is safe."

As they walked along, the missionary asked the boy about
his family. "I'm a Bhil," said the boy, "and nobody loves us."
The missionary said, "I'm here to tell you of somebody who
loves the Bhils very much. In fact, I'm going to be speaking
about that this morning." The kid said, "I can't believe that

story," but he decided to go with the missionary and hear what he had to say. After the meeting, he set the missionary on the right trail and said goodbye.

About a month later, the boy went to a village fair with his father. There they saw a street-corner evangelist. The kid said, "Dad, that guy's telling the same story that the missionary told. Come and listen to it." The father was intrigued by what the evangelist had to say and stayed to talk with him. The evangelist suggested to the father that he send the boy to a mission school. The boy, Joseph Naku, became one of the first people in India to graduate with a medical diploma. He went on to become a major in the army medical corps and was one of my colleagues in Ratlam. His sons, also Christians, are among the leading doctors in central India — all of them Bhils, who normally would have been at the lowest level of Indian society.

Even though it's repeated over and over in the Bible that God loves everyone, we still want to be exclusive, we want to keep him to ourselves. We still have an idea that God is the God of my social club. God is the God of my denomination. God is the God of my race. Every time there's a war, God is the God of our nation. There's a pledge of loyalty to God and the Flag — or the Flag and God. I'm not sure which comes first!

All too often, we find examples of exclusivity right in a church building. One time when I was attending a medical conference in New York, I went with a friend to Riverside Church. There was an announcement that there would be Communion at the end of the service and everyone was welcome to join in. When the service was over, many people started to leave, but we decided to stay for Communion. Two old battleaxes in front of us turned around, raised their eyebrows and asked suspiciously, "Are you of us?" My companion, who was a leprosy worker in Africa, said, "No, we're just medical missionaries."

It was quite a contrast to an Easter Communion service I attended at a Maronnite church in Gaza. In the church there was a slab of rock that was supposed to represent the stone on which Jesus' body was laid out after his crucifixion. The Muslims believed that if a sterile woman crawled under this stone, she would be able to break the hex that was on her. So in the middle of this solemn Easter service Muslim women kept coming through the crowd and struggling to get under this slab. But no one seemed to be disturbed by the commotion.

Then we all stood for communion. There were various Muslim young people standing around the church and just outside the door. When we were finished, and there was bread and wine left over, the Christians in the congregation just passed it to the Muslims. The Christians there knew that the Muslims weren't members of their own faith, but they were celebrating and they wanted to invite their neighbors to celebrate with them. It was quite a shock to me at the time. I was used to asking, "Are they confirmed? Have they joined our church? Is their membership in good standing?" But those Christians didn't care. They had a wonderful fellowship, and they wanted everyone to join in.

The other thing that makes Christianity unique, in my experience, is the fact that we don't place a lot of emphasis on our individual salvation. Probably some people of other faiths think we're semi-pagan because we don't spend enough time thinking about that. But the absolutely indelible, integral part of Christianity is a concern for others. Certainly other religions have provided many great humanitarians, but, in theory at least, the other religions emphasize that one's main job is to get straight with God, and everything else can go by the boards. Christianity says, "No, you're living here on earth, and God is calling you to do something constructive."

One of the big questions in the Christian religion, one that a lot of people get hung up on is, If God is a God of love, if he wants us to show love to everyone around us, how can he allow so much suffering in the world?

Although I've seen some terrible suffering in my lifetime, it never seems to have shaken my faith. I often wonder why, and I have to confess that it's probably because of a very stupid optimism — something I was probably born with. Yet, I really can't explain why God allows these things to happen. And it certainly shakes a person to see tremendous suffering, to see blameless, powerless people suffer. It can make you very cynical. It's one of the things relief agencies have to watch for among their personnel — they may get to the point where they cannot reconcile the suffering they see in a famine or an earthquake with an abounding faith in a loving God.

During the war there certainly were times when a group of us would sit down after the awful devastation of an air raid and say, "We're surprised a thing like this can happen to intelligent people in these modern times — that war, which used to be between people hired to fight, was now blowing apart innocent people, even children, who'd never done anything in their lives." But it was humanity in the mass we blamed, not God.

As I look at history now, I think God had sometimes challenged people with suffering. He's challenged the medical profession with epidemics. He's challenged our economists to see if we can get a better distribution of the world's goods. God works through people, and I think that's how evolution is going to continue to happen. We're not going to have a sudden change, where everyone is good and there is no evil in the world at all. Evil is always there to challenge us, and God permits us to decide whether we're going to choose evil or choose good, whether we're going to take a step backward or a step forward.

I don't feel there's any *assurance* that good is always going to overcome evil, but I also don't believe that the stakes are balanced in favor of evil. My fundamental faith is that good will emerge even from bad situations, that if we follow what is good, we can win. That is why I don't worry too much about whether the church as we know it will survive. I think that, like animals and people, institutions also have to change and adapt. And quite frankly, if the church can't adapt, I think it's doomed.

There are some things in the church that I regard as being good and essential, and there are some things that are just icing on the cake. There's no practice in the church that is, to me, carved in stone. Everything is fluid and adjustable, and I think that's the way we're going to survive.

I can't sympathize with the idea of the church being the Body of Christ on earth, or any similar mystical idea. To me, the church is a fellowship of people who are going in the same direction, and we believe that we will be happier and more effective if we work together. To me, that's all it is. If you're working together, you've got a good church. If you're not working together and you've lost your idealism, then you're not a good church. It's very simple. I don't think the church has a special preserve of sanctity. When the church is doing the right thing, it will have God's blessing and a certain amount of success. And if it's not on the right path, if it becomes inward-looking, then it will not survive. Even if the church as we know it disappears, I believe something good will come from it that can survive.

Certainly there have been times in history when the church has failed. The church failed in Russia, and God passed on the job of bringing about social change to others. But I would rather see evolution than revolution, and I

think the church is essential if we're going to avoid the violence of revolution. The church should be a powerhouse in
development by evolution rather than by revolution. This is
the way it has been in history, and this can be the place of
the church in the future.

For example, we need to see an evolution of compassion
in our urban society. Although I don't think that the church
should be in the business of feeding hungry people in the
city, we can use our influence to insist on a social system
that does not *allow* starvation in a land of plenty. Sometimes
the church can act simply by giving inspiration. Then the
various members of the congregation go out from their
church and carry out their mission at their offices, in political action groups or in whatever they feel called to do.
That's how the whole social service system of Canada was
started, by the CCF party, by people who may not have been
great theologians, but who certainly got their inspiration
from the church.

Yes, attendance figures in the church are declining. And
yes, we live in a fast-changing and sometimes frightening
world. But I have an absolute confidence — I can't explain
how deep it is — that what is good will *not* be destroyed, that
somehow or other what is good in the church and in the rest
of our society will survive, even if the institutions, as we
know them, do not.